It's About You Too

Reducing The Overwhelm For Parents of
LGBTQ+ Kids

Tracy Whitmore

Tracy Whitmore. *It's About You Too: Reducing the Overwhelm for Parents of LGBTQ+ Kids*

This book is dedicated to all the LGBTQ+ young people and their families I've had the privilege to work with over the years, those to come and YOU, the reader.

May your journey be light and uplifted.

Advance Praise

"It's *About You Too* is a warm, gentle, compassionate embrace of the maelstrom of emotions many parents experience as they navigate the unfamiliar terrain of supporting their LGB-TIQ+ child. As the proud parent of a trans child myself and having supported hundreds of parents over the years, I know how vital it is for parents to safely process what can feel like a storm of seemingly conflicting emotions. It can feel really isolating. Tracy Whitmore offers parents practical guidance, tools, exercises and insights to help transform fear into peace and pride for parents of LGBTIQ+ children. This journey requires us to grow, and Tracy has written the book to help parents do just that. So settle down, and allow yourself to absorb the wise and compassionate heart of this work. You're not alone."

~ Rebekah Robertson OAM, Transcend Australia Founder and Proud Mum

"Parents of children (of any age) who come out as LGBTQ+ experience many emotions as they adjust to all the changes happening with their child and their family. As they navigate those changes, it's typical to feel overwhelmed, isolated, and unsure of where to turn for support. What they need most is support for themselves so that they can better support their child, and that's what Tracy excels at. 'It's About You Too' assures parents that their feelings are normal and then gives them tools to help them work through the overwhelm, confusion, grief, guilt, and other emotions they may be experiencing, by sharing stories of people they can relate to. The crown gem is the Moment of Pause (MOP) at the end of each chapter to help you work the stress and emotions out of your body."

~ **Beth Richardson**, Advocate for Parents of Transgender Children. Website: justplainbeth.com

"In *It's About You, Too,* Tracy Whitmore takes a kind and compassionate approach as she guides family members through the complexities of supporting their LGBTQ+ loved ones. This book is a breath of fresh air for those of us who embrace that *The Struggle Is Real, and So Is the Love.*"

~ **Patti Hornstra**, Author of '*When He Was Anna: A Mom's Journey Into the Transgender World.*

"Tracy's support and education for parents in *It's About You Too* is approachable, patient, and compassionate. This book is like getting advice from a friend and will be an immensely helpful resource for anyone supporting queer kids in their lives. I loved the MOPs and action items included in each chapter."

~ **Mandy Giles**, Founder of Parents of Trans Youth

A Felt Experience

"Tracy's advice and support helped me to accept, understand and connect with my LGBTQ young adult child. Our relationship went from estranged and stressful to the loving, connected, and safe relationship a parent longs to have with their child. In the process, I grew in ways that allow me to better parent my other children as well as to accept myself and work through my expectations about my children's adult independence and identity. I now feel confident that I can support my kids as they begin to navigate the world's complex systems on their own, maintaining appropriate boundaries for them and for myself, showing up for them rooted in love and true to my own values."

~ **Alice,** Parent of LGBTQIA+ young adults

Disclaimer

This book is intended to provide educational and informational content. It's not a substitute for professional therapy or mental health support. While this book aims to offer insights, tools, and strategies to enhance personal growth and understanding, it's important to recognise that each individual's circumstances are unique. The intent is to support you to begin your journey and open your mind and heart to your own experiences, feelings and emotions about your child coming out and approach yourself with kindness and compassion. Some topics we discuss may feel confusing, challenging, or confronting. If you're experiencing significant emotional distress, mental health concerns, or require therapeutic assistance, it is strongly recommended that you seek the guidance of a qualified and experienced therapist, counsellor, coach or health professional.

The author and publisher of this book are not liable for any direct or indirect consequences resulting from the application of the material presented. Readers are encouraged to use their own discretion, consult with appropriate professionals, and take personal responsibility for their choices and actions.

Remember, the journey towards personal growth and well-being is multifaceted, and this book should be seen as a supplementary resource, not a replacement for personalised care and expertise provided by social workers, therapists, counsellors, psychologists, or coaches.

Always prioritise your well-being and seek professional assistance when needed.

Note: Indigo Journey's programs are designed to support you on a much deeper level. You can join and take part, alongside reading this book or separately if you're looking for something extra.

Contents

Preface

Hi! I'm Tracy, a Social Worker, Therapist, Coach, and founder of Indigo Journey, who's witnessed hundreds, possibly thousands (but who's counting) of LGBTQ+ young people and their parents' lives affected by how well (or not) their parent managed the news of their child coming out and what follows.

I wrote this book because I was struggling with what I was hearing about parents' experiences when seeking support. All too often, parents of LGBTQ+ people were telling me they were told that "It's not about you. It's about your child and you need to put your feelings aside and support them." This left the parents I speak with, feeling lost, alone, confused and like they were being judged as parents. This resulted in parents withdrawing and not seeking support. It was sad because this is my number one piece of advice for parents. "You don't need to do it alone. Seek support to help you understand your child's experience and process your feelings." I couldn't let this go.

I like to think deeply about things and analyse the details of a situation, and like anything, that can be helpful and other times distracting. I'm also known to think outside the square, to explore the grey in a situation. I'm always that person who, when given two options, will ask, "And what else? Is there another option? Surely there's something else." And there usually is. So, when I asked myself, "Are they right?", the people who say, "It's not about you." The answer was yes AND no.

So, in true Tracy fashion, I decided to explore this further. Yes, others are right when they say, "It's about your child and you need to prioritise them. They need your love and support." However, they're not right when they say, "It's not about you. You need to put your feelings aside."

I don't believe you can ask a parent to turn off their feelings to support their child. Do I want parents to be supportive of their LGBTQ+ child? Yes! Absolutely! It's crucial for their child's well-being. It's simply not possible to turn off your feelings and nor is it healthy to try. The bit in between is the need to explore your feelings, where they're coming from, process them and learn to better understand your child, at the same time as doing your best to support them.

I worked with LGBTQ+ young people and their families for many years. I was witness to both sides of the coin. When families were supportive and when they weren't. When families had the knowledge and the tools to provide the best support possible and those who had the desire but didn't know where to start. As a result of the privilege of walking alongside these families, I decided the next step was to create a service that is solely for parents. I wanted to assist them on their journey of better understanding their and their LGBTQ+ child's emotions and experiences, so they could become their child's number one ally.

Introducing Indigo Journey...

The profound transformations I witnessed in the lives of LGBTQ+ individuals and their families served as the catalyst for me to expand and refine my approach. This led me to develop comprehensive programs and courses aimed at supporting a larger number of families in a more impactful manner. Through this work, I gained invaluable insights into the unique experiences of parents seeking support, allowing me to cultivate a profound understanding that ultimately inspired the conception of 'It's About You, Too'.

Fast forward almost a year, and here we are. I'm so excited to bring this book to you.

How to Use This Book

Your journey will be unique to you and if at any time you feel you could benefit from some extra supports, please don't hesitate to reach out. There are a variety of options for you, including online group and 1:1 coaching programs, DIY courses and other resources. We'll be exploring some potentially tough topics, so I want you to know you don't have to do this alone. Go at your own pace and remember to always be kind to yourself.

Before you get started, I encourage you to grab a notebook and pen to take notes. Find yourself a comfortable, quiet, space to relax with your beverage of choice and carve out some time where you won't be interrupted, so you can delve deep.

You'll find prompts at the end of each chapter to take a Moment of Pause (MOP – the best kind of mop that I'm aware of). MOPs are mini mindfulness exercises designed to support you through each chapter. The intent is to enable you to relax and calm your nervous system, so that you are in the best possible space to explore and learn about your thoughts, feelings, emotions, and experiences.

You'll also find actions or exercises at the end of each chapter. The same as the MOPs, please don't skip them. Give yourself and your child the gift of this experience to consolidate the learning from the reading. In some chapters, the exercise may be related to a section earlier in the chapter. Feel free to jump ahead to the exercise if you feel called to, however, remember to mark your page so you can come back to it.

Take notes, mark the pages you want to come back to and allow yourself the time and space to reflect on how you're feeling, what you're learning and how you want to apply the concepts to your own life.

You may have picked up this book to address a specific need or struggle and get the urge to jump straight to that part of the book. If that's the case, that's perfectly okay, however I'd encourage you to go back and read the rest of the book once you've satisfied that need. You may learn something you didn't know you wanted or needed to learn. Remember, we don't know what we don't know.

Please allow yourself the time and space to complete the MOPs and Actions, as it will set you up for success. In other words, don't skip these bits, they're important. You'll be surprised by the difference they'll make to your experience.

Introduction

Your own personal roadmap

"Be vulnerable to life's lessons – you'll learn quicker"

~ Brené Brown ~

Your child just came out, you're feeling an array of emotions and everyone's telling you, "It's not about you! It's about your child. You need to put your feelings aside and be there for them."

Wow!!! The first time I heard about a parent's experience of this, I was horrified, saddened, and disappointed. Unfortunately, this kind of response is all too common. I knew something had to change. It inspired me to work towards improving the experiences of parents and creating a safe space.

Today, this is your safe space.

Meet Ann

Several years ago, a mother arrived at her session, visibly upset and nervous. I'll call her Ann. She sat there looking at me sheepishly, red-eyed and exhausted. Her child had recently come out as transgender and pansexual. She was so upset, and didn't know how to respond, but knew she had to do something, so she went to see her therapist. Her therapist's response was unhelpful, harsh, and without consideration of the support Ann needed to embark on this journey. Ann was feeling overwhelmed, confused, exhausted, and desperate for help. She was riddled with guilt and shame as a result of the lack of information and support to help her work through her feelings. She sobbed as she told me that everywhere she turned she was being told, "It's not about you", yet she was experiencing powerful emotions and didn't know where to begin.

It was heartbreaking to hear about Ann's experience, to sit with her in her pain, knowing that it didn't have to be like that. This was the day I realised the full impact of the lack of adequate support and encouragement for parents of LGBTQ+ folk. It was something I was already doing; however, I didn't realise my approach was so different from others. I made a mental note on that day, that if we're going to create significant change in the lives of LGBTQ+ young people, we need to start with the parents. It needed to be intentional and not simply left to the already under resourced system in place for supporting LGBTQ+ young people.

Ann had called me the previous day, quite distressed. She shared that her 17-year-old child had told her, the previous week, that they're transgender and pansexual. She wanted to assure me she loves her child, and she knew it wasn't about her, but she was struggling. "I don't even know what pansexual is", she whispered. "I don't know what to think, what to do, or what to say to my child", Ann shared, choking back tears.

She was shocked, confused and overwhelmed, and when she reached out to her therapist, she was told that it wasn't about her and that she must focus on supporting her child. "She said that should be my priority, my child," shared Ann, followed by a deep sigh, "I know she's right, I just don't know how to do that. I'm not a terrible parent. I just don't know how."

The problem was, she didn't know how to support her child. She had so much inner turmoil that she wasn't even sure if she could, even though she desperately wanted to. This is a dilemma that many parents come to me with. I want you to know that it's perfectly normal to feel the way Ann was feeling and it won't feel like that forever.

As I paid more attention, I noticed how common this response to parents was. It was literally coming from everywhere. Health professionals, including mental health professionals, friends, family members and even other parents of LGBTQ+ folk.

The thing is, none of these people mean any harm. In fact, they're all trying to prevent harm to the LGBTQ+ person. And I get it. We all want LGBTQ+ folk to feel safe, loved and supported in their families because that gives them the best chance of living a joyful, successful life. So, I had to ask myself, "Are they right? I mean, everyone's saying it and my priority is also for LGBTQ+ people to live happy, loving, fulfilled lives." It kept niggling at me and the more I heard of these experiences from parents and how it left them feeling, I couldn't let it go, and that's why I decided to write this book.

Families

I'll introduce you to a variety of parents and families throughout this book who've had varying experiences and responded in different ways. Of course, this is only a small glimpse into the experiences of some parents I've worked with, however, I've chosen them specifically with the aim that you'll be able to see a little of yourself in at least one of their stories and take some comfort and feel some hope.

I have, of course, changed everybody's names and altered any identifying elements of their stories to ensure their privacy. If you're reading this and feel like I'm writing about you and I haven't asked your permission, it simply means that your story is similar to others, which is common. For example, I've already had several people reach out to me, after reading my first draft of the introduction, some of whom I'd never met, saying that they felt like I was writing about them.

I'd like to reassure you that every parent mentioned in this book deepened their connection with their child, reduced or eliminated their overwhelm, and became confident, comfortable, and found their voice to advocate for their child in their own way.

The request of parents to put their feelings aside got me thinking about other parenting situations and I realised we don't ask parents to turn off their feelings in other circumstances and just focus on their child. Of course, there are times they need to take a deep breath and 'get the job done'. However, in those circumstances, we still offer compassion.

Just in case you're struggling to believe this to be true or see how it works, we'll explore a couple of those scenarios.

Example 1

When a child is injured or sick – obviously a difficult situation for a parent. To see their child suffering and not be able to take their pain away is heartbreaking for parents. In these circumstances, parents are required to be brave, hold it together and be there for their child, in whatever capacity is necessary. We don't tell the parent that it's not about them, and we don't expect them to ignore their feelings. Most of us will acknowledge how tough it is, offer support, and ask how we can help. We know they can't fall apart in front of their child, but they can with us.

Example 2

A child just won first place in their first National level athletics competition – obviously an exciting experience for the parent, too. A very proud moment. Of course, it is not appropriate for the parent to jump into the limelight and make it all about them. However, again, we wouldn't tell the parent it's not about them. We would congratulate them on their child's win, we'd celebrate with them, we'd listen to them share about all the work and dedication to their child, the car trips to training for the last few years and all the trials and tribulations that got them there. We might even throw them a dinner party to celebrate, as their child goes off and celebrates with their teammates.

Give yourself a break

Parents, I know you're often hard on yourself. You have high expectations of yourself as a parent and you believe your child deserves more than you. However, It Is About You Too. Your and your child's experiences are not mutually exclusive. You are human; you have feelings, thoughts and emotions and they are all valid and require some TLC. Your child needs you to make it about you, too. Your whole family needs you to take better care of yourself, give yourself a break, and allow yourself space to process how you're feeling.

All these people are right. It's not 'all' about you and yes, it is about your child. Yes, you need to get on board and be there for them. They need your unconditional love and support. They want you to embrace them for exactly who they are.

That doesn't mean you have to ignore your own feelings and thoughts. In fact, that'd be detrimental to you, your child, and the rest of your family. In order to be there for your child in the most authentic, effective, loving and supportive way, you have to work through what you're feeling and thinking. It's not possible to effectively shut off those feelings and make it all about your child. Yes, it's true, it's important that you get there as quickly as possible, to minimise the impact on your child. It's also true that you need to do your best to shield your child from your process. As you'll learn throughout this book, they're not the one to learn from or to share your thoughts with.

What would've been a more helpful response from Ann's therapist is, 'It sounds tough and you have a lot of feelings to work through around this. As you may know, it's not your child's responsibility to manage your emotions or be your educator for the parts you don't understand. Let's use our sessions to explore how you're feeling and gather some more information.'

I'm totally aware of why therapists and other health professionals respond the way they do, and I completely understand it. Their focus is to advocate for unconditional love and support for LGBTQ+ folk. I'm also acutely aware that this can be really difficult if a parent is struggling and not able to find the space and support to work through their own emotions, fears and experiences. I'd also like to acknowledge that it's not fair for folk to be put in the position of being the support person and advocate for LGBTQ+ individuals and also providing education, support and understanding for their parents. In other circumstances, it might be considered a conflict of interest. Unfortunately, it seems to be the default at the moment due to a lack of effective alternatives.

What about you

So, your child recently came out and you're confused, overwhelmed and full of emotion. As I said to Ann, this is totally normal. Parenting is one of the hardest, highest pressure jobs you'll ever have. And now there's this to figure out. What do you do? My advice – take a deep breath, make yourself a nice warm beverage of choice and keep reading.

Over the years, I've walked the journey alongside hundreds of parents as they've realised their child's sexuality or gender identity differs from what they expected. I've supported them as they've learned to accept and eventually celebrate their child's sexuality and/or gender identity.

I won't lie. It's not a simple process, however, with patience, kindness and compassion they get there. When they do, they're elated to reach that feeling of unconditionally embracing, loving, supporting, and celebrating their child exactly how they are. This will be you, too.

Like I told Ann, it is about you, too. You matter. Your feelings matter. Your worries and concerns are valid. You can have your feelings and still love your child. Your feelings do not negate your love for your child.

They (feelings) matter. You matter. Your child matters.

When parents arrive at a session with me, they're experiencing an array of emotions, and they're almost always the same. My last client said to me, "Out of the 10 emotions you've got listed on your website, I'm feeling 9 of them..." It's no accident that they're on my website. It's because I commonly hear this from parents and it's a perfectly natural response.

They also ask the same kinds of questions. Wonder the same things. Have the same fears. You're not alone in the way you're feeling. Most parents go through their own version of what you're currently going through.

Are you asking or saying:

- "Is it a phase?"

- "They're too young to know"

- "How can I protect my child?"

- "Did I do something wrong? Something to cause this?"

- "What about grandkids?"

There are a few things I always make clear with my clients and I want to share them with you, too:

1. You matter. It is about you, too. Your thoughts, feelings, and concerns are valid.

2. Your feelings about your child's sexuality or gender identity don't negate your feelings for your child.

3. If you're uncomfortable, they'll see straight through you. You can't fool your child. Get comfortable as quickly as you can, so you can connect with your child and deepen your relationship with them.

I know this isn't easy, but I also know you can do this, and it doesn't need to take months and years. You have a choice;

continue to listen to unhelpful advice from people who may or may not have your child's best interests at heart, OR read this book to find out how you can continue to prioritise your child AND work through your own feelings and take care of your own needs. In fact, you'll find out how prioritising yourself has much better results for your child, family, and relationships.

What are you going to choose?

Please be assured;

'You **Do** Matter,' 'It **Is** About You, Too' **AND** it's time to work through this together.

- This book is for you, if you are a parent, carer or guardian of an LGBTQ+ person, regardless of their age and are:

- Struggling with their sexuality or gender identity

- Finding your own feelings, thoughts and emotions difficult

- Feeling shame, guilt, fear or anger

- Not sure where to turn and feeling stuck between your feelings for your child and your faith, beliefs, values, or thoughts.

- Confused or uncertain about what your child has shared with you

- Tired of being told it's not about you

- Wanting to support your child and simply unsure about

the best way to do that? Perhaps you're wishing this would all just go away, or maybe you're feeling ok with your child's sexuality or gender identity but feeling some feelings that are not comfortable or what you would've expected of yourself. Regardless, there's something in here for you.

It's also for you if you're a family member of an LGBTQ+ person and feeling any of the above or want to support someone who is.

You'll also benefit from reading this book if you're a professional who supports LGBTQ+ people and/or their families.

In this book, we'll explore the experiences, feelings, struggles, beliefs, values and thought processes that lead to a sense of overwhelm, isolation, confusion and often despair. Just like Ann, you're likely to be feeling an array of emotions and perhaps don't understand why or where they're all coming from.

You might be asking yourself, "Why do I need to read this? I'm fine. Shouldn't I just get my child a therapist?" The simple answer is, no, your child needs you to be ok. Well, actually, they need you to be better than okay. I don't know if your child needs a therapist, however, I know that when a child's parents are doing well, when they're able to completely understand their own feelings, experiences and emotions and can heal where healing is required, they are much more able to be present for their child. Your child needs you to do this. And don't you want to be the best parent you can be? Unconditionally loving, supporting, embracing and celebrating your child, exactly how they are?

This will be a journey of learning, growing, healing, connection both to self and your child and developing the skills to prioritise yourself without sacrificing your family. In fact, your family will thrive as a result of you prioritising yourself. And who doesn't want that for their family?

A little housekeeping

One of the common struggles I hear from parents is the difficulty in understanding and/or remembering all the different labels and language now used. I've done my best to keep it simple. However, I've also included a Glossary of Terms at the back to help you along. Please understand that while I've done my best to provide a clear, accurate glossary, the terminology used by and for LGBTQ+ folk is changing all the time, so use this as a guide. It's more important to listen to what your child and other LGBTQ+ folk tell you about themselves and their identities.

You'll hear people, including me, use a range of umbrella terms to refer to people who identify as not heterosexual or cisgender (cis - people who identify with the gender they were assigned at birth). This includes, but is not limited to, shortening the initialism, LGBTQ+, a different order of the letters, and the word queer. They're all valid and simply depend on the individual's preference. It's important to acknowledge that while the term 'queer' is now broadly used within the LGBTQ+ community, it's still offensive and upsetting to some people, so please be mindful if you use it.

As mentioned above, there'll be plenty of opportunities to pause, reflect, breathe, take part in an exercise and, perhaps the most important, give yourself a hug. These elements are just as important as the rest of the book. They may feel challenging if it's not what you're used to, however, 'challenges' often result in the most profound growth and learning. Do your best to embrace yourself, your experience, and all your emotions with loving kindness and compassion.

MOP – Moments of Pause

Now let's check out the MOPs (Moment of Pause) that'll be at the end of each chapter. As I mentioned, they're as important as the rest of the book, so please give them the attention they deserve. Or should I say... Allow yourself the attention, time and space that you deserve. Give yourself this gift.

I won't pretend this is an easy journey, but I will tell you that you're in the right place, and you will get there. Quicker and more easily than you expect.

One thing you'll notice is that I place a lot of value on self-care and this journey with you is no different. When we're going through challenging times, we often forget the most important things. What we need to keep our strength up, keep us well, and keep our mind functioning at its full capacity. Don't get me wrong, I'm not suggesting that doing a little mindfulness, breathing, exercise and eating well is going to make all your troubles go away and everything all rosy again. But these MOPs will make them more approachable. They'll be your little reminder to breathe, to take a moment for yourself, to ensure your cup is getting filled up, so that you have the best chance possible at getting through this time as quickly and seamlessly as possible.

Please make these a priority for your and your family's sake. For some of you, I know, there'll be a little voice in the back of your head saying, "You don't need this. It won't make any difference. Just skip to the parts you need." To that voice, I say, "Ssshhhh, so far, your way hasn't reduced the pain or overwhelm, so let's try something different. What harm can it do? After all, you're breathing anyway." And to be honest, in the time it took to read that paragraph you could've already experienced some benefits from intentional breathing or other mini-mindfulness practices.

So what do you say? You trusted me enough to buy this book, so let's give it a go.

Your first MOP ~ Trust your heart and your body

The Sigh

Introducing... The sigh - it's our body's natural way to release and encourage a deeper, healthier breath.

Take a deep breath in and let out a big sigh.

It can be as loud as you like. Don't hold back.

Repeat two more times.

Notice how that feels. Do a quick scan of the body. Do you notice anything different?

There may be no noticeable change, it may be subtle, and it may be significant. Either way, all is okay.

If it feels helpful, write what you notice in your journal.

You may notice we all sigh at different times in our lives. It's usually a subconscious action in response to something challenging. What you might not notice is that we also sigh when our breath has been short and shallow.

We sometimes take a sigh as a sign that there is something wrong with someone, that they're annoyed, angry or frustrated. This may be the case, however, not always. Either way, it's our body's way of helping us out. It's releasing some tension, encouraging us to let go a little, and supporting us to breathe a little deeper. In order to sigh (a big breath out), we have to take a big breath in. The result... At least one deep breath, which your body will be very grateful for.

You've got this! See you in chapter one.

Chapter 1

The Struggle Is Real, And So Is The Love

Building Your Awareness

"Why do you like thunderstorms?"

" Because it shows that even nature needs to scream some-times"

~ E.D.~

Let's be honest

As this chapter title suggests, I want to acknowledge that the struggle is genuine. You may relate to some or all the struggles I talk about; please take what feels helpful and resonates with you. I want to assure you that your struggles do not reflect your love for your child. I know as well as you do that you love your child and want what's best for them.

You may be wondering how I know this. It's easy! You wouldn't be here if you didn't.

You're here because you love your child and want to be the best parent you can be, and at this moment in time, you're finding it difficult to know how to do that. Or perhaps you're nervous that you can't because of your feelings and thoughts. Many parents I work with also feel torn between their struggle to support their child and their fear that if they do, that may also be harmful.

Please know that this is all very normal. When confronted with any life changing situation It is impossible for our brain to simply make a decision and promptly change. We simply do not work that way. Everybody must go through a psychological process this is particularly true when the change is confronting and or challenging. Not only do we need to move through these stages it is normal to oscillate revisiting earlier stages. It is important to realise this is healthy and facilitates emotional growth. The process often begins with denial. I'd like you to understand that denial, while tough for your child, is your brain's way of protecting you when it's unable to take in confronting information. Regardless of how supportive (or unsupportive) you feel right now, the very act of working through your feelings helps you to come out the other side much stronger and with a deeper connection with your child. Throughout this book, we'll explore and delve deep into your thoughts, feelings, values, beliefs and emotions. Where they might come from, and what to do about them.

For now, what thoughts, feelings, emotions, beliefs, and values are we speaking about? Any parent who reads my website completes my courses and programs, follows me on social media or has a conversation with me, will tell you that they didn't realise just how many different elements can be at play, fuelling a debilitating sense of overwhelm, fear and worry. They expected it would be a lot, but it was eye-opening and validating for them once we began to go through them all.

Before we delve deeper, let's look at some of the feelings we discuss in the upcoming chapters. Keep in mind these are not in any particular order, as these feelings can come up at different times and sometimes circle back.

Put your hand up if any of these ring a bell for you.

- Overwhelmed– I guess we've already agreed on this one.

- Fear, worry, & concern – I know there are so many things you might be afraid of or worried about. Your child's safety, future, education, career, health, and well-being are just a few.

- Grief & loss – yes, grief is a normal part of the process.

- Guilt

- Embarrassment & shame

- Anger

- Denial, Disbelief or doubt

- Confusion

- Disappointment

- Shock

- Sadness

One parent I spoke to recently said, "I looked at your website and ticked off 9 of the 10 emotions you have listed there". I get told this often.

If you relate to their response, it's important to acknowledge you're not alone in how you feel; you don't have to go through this alone. There are thousands of parents out there struggling with the same or similar thoughts, feelings and experiences as you. While that doesn't necessarily take away your struggles, you can take comfort in knowing that because others feel similarly, it is perfectly normal, and there are solutions. More importantly, there are also thousands of parents who have moved through the process and are feeling more fulfilled and connected.

Riding the rollercoaster

I've worked with hundreds of parents who began at a similar stage to you, whether that's when their child first came out or some time down the track when they were still struggling and or a new struggle had arisen. They were overwhelmed and unable to see a way through, not knowing where to start or how to shift their thoughts and/or feelings. There were so many thoughts and emotions it was hard to see the forest for the trees. It's important to note that you cannot grow through these feelings by simply flicking a switch.

Parents go through stages, similar to the stages of grief, Everyone's experience is unique to them. You may recognise some of these stages. You may feel like you oscillate between a couple, and it is important to recognise this is normal. We'll talk more about these in later chapters, but here is a brief overview of how they look. It's also important to note that the starting point can be different for everyone, too.

- Denial/Confusion – Feelings of Disbelief, anger, shock, and overwhelm

- Fear – worry, concern, grief/loss, sadness

- Shame – Embarrassment, disappointment, guilt, regret

- Acceptance – Confidence, clarity, love and support

- Celebration – Pride, unconditional love and support

I know you (like other parents I work with) want the best for your child. You want to be a loving, supportive parent. You want to be the best parent you can be. The good news is that you can be, and you will be. You need to allow yourself the time and space to work through the process, including your old perceptions of how things were. You might be grieving the son/daughter you thought you had, or the hopes of grandchildren, among other things. Yes, you still have your child; however, for many parents, grief is a significant element of this process, and it's essential to acknowledge and respect it.

Aside from reading this book and accessing one-on-one support, becoming part of a community with people who can relate to your experiences and share their solutions can be a valuable part of this process. That's exactly why I created a beautiful community of parents to be there for each other, to be a 'virtual ear'. It's a space where families can know they are seen, heard, understood and embraced. We'd love you to join us. (You can get the link from my Instagram bio or email me. My Instagram handle is @tracy.indigojourney)

Meet Josie and Paul

Like Ann, Josie came to see me feeling distressed and over-whelmed. Her 28-year-old son had recently come out to her as gay. She was confused because he'd had girlfriends before and, in her words, "he's a blokey bloke". She shared that "he loved his cars, worked in a traditionally masculine job, loved to play footy and was overall very masculine, with a good group of blokey friends." Josie expressed that she was aware that these were all heterosexual stereotypes. While she didn't want to perpetuate any stereotypes of the gay community, these were all the reasons that influenced her assumptions about him being straight.

Paul, Josie's son, had moved away in his early 20s because he could not continue hiding who he was. He didn't want to disappoint his Mum and was unsure how the rest of the family would feel. He was the only male offspring, so he was carrying the responsibility of maintaining the family name, among other things. He knew people saw him in a particular way and expected certain things from him, and being gay was not one of them.

Josie was oscillating between shame and denial.

On one hand, she felt guilty about not realising her son was gay, not being more in tune with how he was feeling when he was younger. She felt both sad and ashamed that she was not there for him to support him during his adolescent years when he was coming to realise his sexuality.

On the other hand, she continued to refer back to all the stereotypical signs indicating he was straight and maybe just confused because his last girlfriend broke his heart. "He was shattered, totally broken when she left him", she would tell me.

This denial helped her to manage the sometimes unbearable guilt and shame. She would sit in my office, crying inconsolably, mumbling through the tears and heaving chest, "What kind of mother doesn't know? What kind of mother doesn't notice these things? Surely there were signs. I was too caught up in my own stuff to notice that my son was struggling." "Maybe there was too much female influence around him. If only I'd worked harder to keep his father around. Why didn't I try to expose him to more male role models? I was too soft with him. I should've roughed him up a bit."

Paul had 3 sisters and his father left when he was young and didn't show any interest in being part of his kids lives. He had been quite abusive towards Josie, and this was a traumatic time for her. She was blaming herself for the separation, for Paul's father abandoning him, and for somehow causing Paul to be gay.

We'll go into this more in later chapters; however, I want to be clear – no one causes a person to be gay. And when Josie was able to calm her nervous system down (she practised the same breathing exercise we'll do at the end of this chapter), she could see how contradictory her feelings and thoughts were. She blamed herself for Paul not having the opportunity to develop his masculinity, which she believed to be the cause of his sexuality; however, she also shared that his masculinity was the key reason she has struggled to believe he's gay and why she was so shocked when he came out.

We don't think clearly when we're distressed, afraid, and over-whelmed. The stress in our system interferes with our mind's ability to see things clearly, process accurately, think logically and make helpful decisions. This highlights the importance of self-care, of finding an activity that allows your system to quieten and calm. As I mentioned earlier, we'll explore various strategies throughout this book. You'll find a new one at the end of each chapter (MoPs). I encourage you to try them all and then pick the ones that feel good to you, to take with you, throughout your life, for whenever you need a little calm.

You're not alone

I want to reassure you that you are not alone in your experience, thoughts and feelings. The simple fact that I can write about them here proves that your experience is not unusual. Of course, there'll be variations to how you experience your child coming out; however, most parents of LGBTQ+ kids go through a similar process with minor deviations.

I know this doesn't take away your struggles, but hopefully, you can feel reassured that there is a community of people ready to support you and that you're heading in the right direction.

You only need to scour the internet (carefully, as the internet is renowned for surprises), and see the array of parent groups across the globe, to know that many parents are struggling and looking for extra support. Anyone who experiences a significant change or challenge in their life does better when their story is shared by someone who has walked a similar path or had a similar objective. As I will likely say many times before this book ends, "It is important not to do this alone; look for appropriate support to guide, hear and see you".

I've worked with many parents who wished they'd met me months or years beforehand so that they could've ended their struggles much sooner. This was one of the driving forces behind the creation of this book. I hope that it reaches every parent exactly when they need it. When they're ready to take the next step. Is this you? Are you prepared to take the next step? I guess yes, and that's why you picked up this book. Let's do this together.

Meet the families.

You've already met Ann in the introduction and Josie and Paul here in this one, and now I'll share a bit of a snapshot of who else you're going to meet throughout this book. This is a reminder that all families' names have been changed, and any other identifying elements have been altered to ensure their privacy. As I mentioned, my goal is that you recognise a little of yourself in some of these stories and take some solace in knowing there is hope things can shift.

Alison

In chapter two, you'll meet Alison, a mother of 3 who already felt overwhelmed with her busy schedule and all the demands on her time and energy. When her child came out as trans, she had no idea how she or her family could cope.

Jackie

I'll introduce you to Jackie in chapter 3, whose son came out as bisexual but didn't want his father to know. You'll hear about the struggles of keeping a secret from her husband. Her story illustrates the importance of respecting your child's trust and how to navigate this type of situation.

Jason

You'll also meet Jason in chapter 3, who's worried about how his workplace will react to his son being gay. He believed there was a significant chance he would be sacked, miss opportunities for promotion or need to resign because it became a toxic environment.

Cassie & Brody

In chapter four, you'll meet Cassie & Brody. Cassie is a mother of a gender-diverse 15-year-old. Brody's gender identity shifted several times during the time I worked with Cassie. This made it more difficult for her to understand what was going on, believe Brody and manage her own emotions enough to continue being supportive.

Peter & Shelly

You'll also meet Peter & Shelly in chapter four. Shelly came out as gay when she was 16 years old and Peter managed fairly well. However, now as a 32 year old, she is making some big life decisions, and Peter is finding them difficult. Peter's current challenges have highlighted some underlying struggles he originally ignored, which were being informed, subconsciously through his beliefs and values. They all came to the surface when Shelly shared that she was getting married.

Lauren & Jake

Lauren & Jake will join us in chapter five. Jake came out as gay, originally at age 8 and then again at age 11. Lauren struggled to know if he was old enough to know or even understand his sexuality.

Sarah

In chapter six, you'll meet Sarah, whose gay child later came out as trans and Sarah was caught off guard by how strong her feelings were about it. She was proud of being the 'supportive, advocate' Mum beforehand and was overwhelmed by an array of unexpected emotions when her child came out as trans.

Sally & Jay

I introduce Sally & Jay in chapter seven. Sally's child, Jay, came out as trans when they were 14, and Sally was convinced it was a phase and that Jay was just a tomboy, just like she was at that age.

Cynthia, Geoff & Thomas

In chapter nine, you'll meet a new family and revisit two others.

Last but not least, let me introduce you to Cynthia and Geoff, who are the parents of 15-year-old Thomas, who they had suspected of being gay for a long time. They supported Thomas; however, due to his coming out, they decided to implement some new household rules that didn't go down too well with Thomas.

I want to acknowledge there are many sexual orientations and gender identities not represented in these stories; however, the experiences of parents are still similar. I'd also like to acknowledge the intersectional experiences of individuals, like race, class, religion, and disability, among others, that are not made clear in these stories. These intersections can have a significant impact on parents and their child's experiences, interactions, and the processing of their feelings. Please know this is the beginning of the journey, and there are processes to help you work through the different layers of discrimination or disadvantage. Please reach out if you'd like extra support.

Feel what you feel, AND do the work.

You can have all of these feelings and love your child at the same time - worry, sadness, anger, fear, disbelief, confusion, all of them. It's important to keep front of mind these feelings do not negate your love for your child. Regardless of what you've been told, your feelings matter; they are valid and need space. As we mentioned above they're a necessary part of your growth. Take the time you need and take action to move towards how you want to feel. I'm here to support you through those steps.

Too many parents I've worked with and had conversations with, report being told, often in quite a harsh manner, "It's not about you". It's even been implied or stated outright that they're bad parents for having the struggles they have. For feeling the way they feel. This is simply unhelpful and implies a fundamental misunderstanding of how our psyche works.

As mentioned earlier, these comments come from every-where, including health and mental health professionals. I know what these professionals are trying to do. I understand where they're coming from. I've worked with thousands of LGBTQ+ young people and witnessed the pain and suffering when their parents are not supportive, reject, abuse, and dis-own them. It is a hard pill to swallow. This provides a bit of a fire in the belly of the health professionals supporting LGBTQ+ people to ensure parents know they must 'get it right' for their kids. Those professionals are right in some ways, it's not your child's problem. It's not for them to sort out or help you through. It's not your child's responsibility to educate or make you feel better. Your struggles are not for their ears or hearts. They're also right when they say, you need to support your child.

I'm also passionate about LGBTQ+ people being supported by their parents because I know the life-saving difference it makes. And from my experience, I also understand that in order to do this, parents need to be supported through their process, which is why I work differently. I know for you to be the best parent you can be, you need the space to be able to express your struggles, your thoughts and feelings openly. It would be best if you had a place that is safe and non-judgmental, where you can move through these feelings so that you can get to the other side as quickly as possible.

I want to be clear; this is not permission for anyone to stay where they are, feeling stuck and overwhelmed by these feelings. Nor is it an excuse to continue not responding well to their child. It's not a green light for parents to expect their child to accept their feelings or to fix them. This is an opportunity for you to be seen, heard and understood while you explore your experience and learn to understand your child better and work your way to a place of peace where you can love and support your child unconditionally, exactly how they are. And I know that's precisely why you're here.

It takes time

It can feel like a juggling act for a little while. You might feel like you're living two lives, which may feel uncomfortable. Feeling uncomfortable is okay; it is your new normal for a time. Ever heard the saying – "Life begins outside your comfort zone"? You've heard new information about your child you were perhaps not expecting, so it makes sense that you're feeling discomfort. Being uncomfortable is better than hurting or burdening your child. So, let's get comfortable with being uncomfortable for a while.

The key is that you realise that your struggles are valid; it is about you, too, because you love your child deeply and want the best for them, and there are steps you can take to move through how you're feeling right now, into a space of peace, comfort and love. Remember, everything is temporary, including how you're feeling right now.

MOP ~ Trust your heart and your body

Extended exhale

We're going to expand on the 'sigh' from the introduction.

Find a comfortable seat. (though this can be done anytime, anywhere)

The extended exhale is exactly how it sounds. Your exhale is going to be longer than your inhale. Ideally, double the length.

Begin by taking a deep breath in for the count of four and without holding your breath, shift straight into your exhale.

Exhale for the count of eight.

Inhale for the count of four, and exhale for the count of eight.

Repeat eight more times.

It might be helpful to imagine your holding a straw in your mouth for the exhale.

Blow into the straw to help extend your exhale, until your breath is completely gone.

You can either count 10 rounds or time yourself for two minutes. They're about equal.

After just 2 minutes, your nervous system has calmed, and your body has relaxed, at least a little.

Notice what you feel...

If it feels helpful, write it in your journal.

This now allows you to be much more able to take in what you're reading and participate in the activities. Our mind's capability to absorb new information increases significantly when we're calm, our nervous system isn't working overtime, and we're not anxious. For this reason, I'd encourage you to start to make this a part of your regular practice. As I said, you can do this anytime, anywhere and no one needs to know.

Notice what you feel...

If it feels helpful, write it in your journal.

Take Action ~ You've got this!

What you already know

Acquire yourself a journal or notebook that you can dedicate to this process.

Find a quiet, comfortable space (if you haven't already) to read, where you won't be interrupted.

In your journal record the following:

- Other difficult things you've worked through in the past. (when you've felt overwhelmed, stressed, out of your depth, upset, afraid, worried etc.)

- What are some things you did that were helpful?

- Write some things that were unhelpful.

- Take a moment to reflect – can you see any of these things being helpful in your current situation? If so, highlight those. If not, that's ok, that's why we're here to figure this out together.

Turn to a blank page and write yourself a love note. You can use my words, or create your own.

Dear (insert your name),

I acknowledge things are tough right now. I know you're feeling (insert the feelings you're experiencing). I also know that you are strong, resilient, smart and loving, so you will get to the other side. You'll use your resources to do what's best for you and your family. In fact, you've already started, by reading this book.

Give yourself some love and kindness. Allow yourself some space and commit your heart to be open to learning and healing.

You've got this!

Love, kindness and compassion, from (insert your name)

Key points

- The struggle is temporary

- You're on a journey, it's a process

- You don't have to do this alone

- It's Not Your Child's Responsibility to Educate or Support You

- Your feelings don't negate your love

- Feel your feelings, love your child, do the work

Chapter 2

Managing The Overwhelm

Self-Care Is Crucial

"Don't dwell in the past, do not dream of the future, concentrate the mind on the present moment"

~ Buddha ~

When your child first comes out, it can feel like a lot. A significant amount of information to take in, many emotions swishing around and considerable expectations from your child, yourself, and others.

"I feel so overwhelmed" is the most common statement I hear from parents. I hear it so often and it has such an impact on parents I felt it deserves its very own chapter. We'll begin by exploring some causes of the overwhelm, then we'll touch on some of the science and physiology around it and finish with some answers, suggestions, guidance and tips and strategies to move through them.

Please note, I don't consider these suggestions a replacement for personalised, specialised support from a therapist or coach, however it's a fantastic place to start, to ease some of that overwhelm.

I like the online dictionary Meriam Webster definition of overwhelmed - "completely overcome or overpowered by thought or feeling". I feel like many parents I work, or have worked with, would agree. This definition fits with their descriptions of their experiences and feelings.

I know, because you're here reading this book, and because it's the truth for most parents, you want the best for your child. You want them to be safe, happy, and living an enjoyable, successful, fulfilled life. I want to assure you, with the right support and unconditional love, they have a greater chance of living to their potential, overcoming hurdles and flourishing. Let's bust this overwhelm together, so you can show up for your family as you would like to.

I understand your child's sexuality and/or gender identity is new to you, or you've known for a while, and that you are struggling. Perhaps it was a big surprise, or maybe you had a sense, and this confirmation has thrown you. Are you feeling confused, worried, or a bunch of conflicting emotions and thoughts? And all of this is on top of your ordinary life experiences and parenting expectations. Any wonder it feels like too much. There's a good reason you're feeling overwhelmed. We'll go into the emotions, thoughts, concerns, and experiences in more detail throughout this book, however for now, we'll focus on establishing strategies to manage these emotions. Please come back to this chapter at any time it feels helpful.

Remember to breathe...

Let's be honest. Every human has their limits and although you may like to think you're invincible, you're not, you're human. You have limits too. Whether you've found yours, or they're just around the corner, the truth is, you can't pour from an empty cup, so if your cup is running low or empty, you can no longer give. Let me repeat that because you need to hear it. You cannot pour from an empty cup. Have you ever felt like you've got nothing left to give? Like you're depleted, emotionally, mentally and/or physically? That is an indicator that your cup is empty. If you're continuously giving and/or doing for others, you'll run out of steam, energy, and strength, whether that is emotional, physical, or both. Stress, isolation, rejection, fighting, rejection, illness, and fatigue can also drain your cup.

Fill your own cup first!

In order to show up as the best parent, partner, friend, colleague and person you can be, you need to fill your own cup first. This means stop and recharge your batteries, to replenish your emotional, mental, and physical energy. If your cup is full and you keep filling it, you will create overflow and you can give from there, the overflow in the saucer. That way your cup will always be full, and you'll never be at risk of running out. You will have more to give to your loved ones.

I often get asked one or all the following, "how do I stop the overwhelm?", "How do I get through this overwhelm?" or "I have no idea what to do next, I'm so overwhelmed. Where do I even start? Life was already hectic. How can I even begin to deal with this?" Any of these resonate with you?

Taking care of yourself means it's crucial to find at least some small moments to check in with yourself and do something that brings you joy. That will mean different things for different people, but we all have something. If you haven't done it for a while, it might take some thought to remember what that might be. If it's not something you're used to, start small. It might require you to ask for some help, delegate a task or two, or even say no every so often. Our MOPs at the end of each chapter are a great place to start. Keep reading and you'll find some examples of what other parents have done to ease their burden of overwhelm.

Filling your own cup first requires you to do something that parents are often not so good at and that is putting yourself first sometimes. For some of you that might feel like a swear word, or others might say, "I put myself first sometimes". If you're like one parent I met several years ago, we need to talk. She told me she got some 'me time' every second week when her kids spent the afternoon at her mothers. When I asked her what she did while the kids were at her mothers, she said, "I do the grocery shopping, change the bed sheets, catch up on the washing and clean the bathrooms and floors. It's fantastic, because I get everything done without interruptions or someone walking on the wet floor or demanding I buy them something at the grocery store." I realise getting these things done without interruption can definitely be a contributor to reducing overwhelm. But let's be clear, this is NOT 'me time', it is NOT self-care, it is NOT bringing you joy. Relief maybe, but not joy. And this is not what I'm talking about when I say, "fill your own cup".

Origins of overwhelm?

Reducing overwhelm, we first need to figure out all contributing factors and they're likely to be coming from a variety of directions. Some related to your child's recent coming out and others about something completely separate.

A feeling of overwhelm occurs when the expectations on us are larger than we have capacity for. Those expectations may come from you, from others, or many other things. In fact, that's often the case. However, what I also notice, within myself and others, is that we're often misguided in where those expectations and stressors are coming from. We often think they're coming from others when we might be actually placing those expectations on ourself. Figuring out where the often many elements of overwhelm are coming from can be an empowering process, because if it is coming from yourself, or at least some of it is, you have the power to change it. Keep in mind, the sources of some stressors may remain in your unconscious, for now.

I also want to acknowledge that, in families, overwhelm can have a multitude of contributing factors. There's work, household chores and responsibilities, parenting, financial concerns and commitments, partners expectations and needs, extended family, and the general 'juggling life' factor. When something new is added, it can feel like it's more than you can manage. You may feel like it's that new thing (in this case your child coming out) that you need to address to reduce the overwhelm, and in many ways, that is true. However, I often find that it feels easier, quicker, and more approachable for parents to look at all elements of overwhelm, particularly the more familiar things, first, because this can help to make space for this new experience.

It's like anything new, it can feel impossible in the beginning. Take labels and terminology in the LGBTQ+ space. There has definitely been a significant shift in the last 10 years, and it can feel hard to keep up with, understand or learn. A quick note on language; I'd like to reassure you that you don't have to know it all. You don't have to understand it. The first and most important step is to hear what your child is telling you, how are they describing themselves and the way they feel. If they use a label, then great, you can also use that label. If they don't, they may not be ready or interested in a label. Do your own research to get the bigger picture and then simply go with what they're telling you. I have a glossary of terms on my website (indigojourney.co) to help you along but remember, you don't have to learn it all.

Back to the source of your expectations and stressors. Take a moment to reflect. Where do you think yours are coming from? It's easy to say, "it's because my kid just dropped a bombshell on me. They're gay and I'm never going to have grandkids." Or "My son just told me they're bisexual. What does that mean for their future? Does that mean they'll never have a committed relationship?" Or "My kid just told me they're trans and I have no idea what that will mean for them or our family. I don't know how to support them, or if I should try to stop them. What if they're wrong? What if they make these decisions and change their mind later?" "And amongst all that, I'm trying to run a household, continue to show up at work and do my job effectively, and my family still expects dinner on the table every night."

I feel overwhelmed just writing this, so I can only imagine how it feels for you. Well actually, I can do more than imagine. I've definitely had my own versions of these thoughts and feelings over the years as I parented and co-parented five kids. Any parent can insert their own version of the above and, for parents of LGBTQ+ folk, there's an added layer.

I could suggest that these expectations often come from within the individual, including subconsciously. I know this might be hard to hear or even believe. Back when my kids were teenagers, I certainly didn't feel like this was the case. Though, I now understand that it was my thoughts and expectations that created and/or exacerbated my overwhelm. We're not looking to blame, because there is no fault. It is a normal human response and automated brain functioning. This trick is to learn to notice when this is happening, observe, reflect and acknowledge. The good news is, when we can recognise and acknowledge the elements of the overwhelm that are coming from within us, we have more opportunity to shift it and with practice, minimise the overwhelm. The alternative, which is coming from an external place, is much harder to shift because we can't control other people. We only have control over our own responses and behaviours. Recognising that we have some control over the overwhelm is the most empowering experience.

One way I help my clients figure this out is to do a big brain dump of what they feel is creating the overwhelm and spend some time reflecting. To be honest, I've used this same strategy myself many times. I find when we make the time for ourselves to get clear on what we're feeling, how our thoughts are affecting the way we're feeling and explore strategies to make minor changes, the trickle effect takes over. When I practice this myself, I notice things shifting all around me and that's exactly what my clients, friends, and colleagues report back to me, too. (I take you through this exercise in the Take Action, section at the end of this chapter)

Alison

A perfect example of the big brain dump that comes to mind is a mother I worked with about 12 months ago, Alison. Before her child came out as trans, she already felt like she lived a busy life. Both parents worked full time, the kids were in school and the whole family had extracurricular activities after school and on weekends. Between them (2 adults and 3 kids, aged 11, 14 & 16) they played several sports, used the gym, swam, played 3 musical instruments, and were all involved in martial arts. In addition, both parents had aging parents who lived close by, and they liked to do what they could to help them.

When Alison's child came out, before she could even process what this all meant, it hit her that this was another thing she needed to do. Her initial reaction was in response to the practical steps that might occur. Well, at least those that first came to mind, with the limited knowledge she had. She felt that was too much. She already felt like she was bursting at the seams, and she couldn't fathom finding the extra time for appointments and all the other things that she was cognisant of not knowing, let alone her own emotional processing.

She contacted me, realising she had little information about what might be needed, but what she knew was she already felt like she was at capacity, so couldn't do it alone. Alison and her family were very grateful the GP passed on my details. I was able to help Alison put the many facets of her life into perspective. Give her some simple answers and accurate information and together we did the above activity so she could reduce the overwhelm.

Please note, everyone will start from their own place. Every tiny step forward is a movement in the right direction and is a win. This is where Alison was on her own journey.

Alison shared that her overwhelm was reduced by about 50% after just a couple of appointments. That's how useful this process can be. What Alison was able to realise was that she was taking on a lot of responsibility that she didn't need to. Some of those things she continued for now, and some she changed. The key was that she realised she was making the choice. No one was forcing her. This lifted a tremendous weight off her shoulders and made space for her to think about how she could best support her trans child.

Below is a list of some choices she made.

- Cook dinner less: - she was cooking 7 nights a week because she thought she had no choice. When she realised other family members could benefit from learning and practising cooking, she delegated the task 3 nights a week. Now her partner and 2 oldest children cook once a week. That frees up Alison's time and energy 3 nights a week. She's now able to enjoy cooking again. Alison has also made a note to explore meal planning in the future when this new plan settles into being a habit for the family.

- Share transport to sports and other activities: - Alison felt like she had to be at every activity for the whole time, therefore she might as well drive them. She had lost the enjoyment of watching her children's sport and other activities. It had become a burden because she was feeling overstretched. This, of course, translated to guilt. She realised she had a lot more choices than she thought. Her husband had offered to do some of the transport and so had other parents, but she felt like a 'bad mum' if she wasn't there. Her solution was to accept her partner's offer and carpool with a couple of other parents. This meant she had the freedom and flexibility to not watch sometimes or to attend for part of a game, rather than the whole thing. For example, her partner or another parent might do the drop-off and she could get there a little later to pick them up and catch the end of the game.

- Delegate some household chores: - it surprised me to

hear how much, or should I say, how little anyone else was doing in such a busy household. Alison grew up with a mother who worked between 5 and 10 hours a week outside of the home and therefore took care of most of the household chores. Alison believed, to be a good mum and partner, she also needed to do the same. Except Alison had a full-time job and a lot of other responsibilities. It wasn't physically feasible for her to expect to do all that her mum did. Alison shyly admitted that her mum had been trying to tell her this for years.

A little reluctantly, Alison created a basic schedule that handed over some simple responsibilities to other family members. After about a month, she said it began to feel good. She could see the benefits for everyone. It was empowering for her children, earning extra pocket money by taking on more responsibility, they felt more independent, and she had increased energy to be more present in her relationships with her family and at work. She also shared, jokingly, it turns out her husband knows how to fold washing. His Mum taught him.

These simple changes weren't easy for Alison at first, however, the benefits were incredible for her and her family. And this was only the beginning. Reducing the overwhelm in other areas of her life allowed her more space to explore how she was feeling and what needed to happen in relation to her child's gender identity. Yes, it was still tough, but not as debilitating as it originally felt. She created some breathing space to have a conversation about how she was feeling about her child's gender, which led to her being able to explore the possible next steps for her child.

What has become apparent to me, over the years, is that parenting can be an overwhelming job at times and finding out your child is LGBTQ+ can be enough to feel like it takes you to your limits or perhaps even tips you over the edge. Going through the process of understanding your child's sexuality and/or gender identity and your thoughts and emotions that are attached to that takes time. It can feel like you don't have that time, space, or energy. You're still running a household, and you have other kids that need you and your employer, while they might be understanding, still need you to do your job well.

None of this means you love your child any less. It's just feeling like a lot at the moment. That's why we first look at where in your life we can make some adjustments, either temporary or permanent, to reduce the overwhelm. Essentially, giving you some breathing space.

A snapshot into the science and physiology of stress

Why is 'breathing space' so important? This is key to you being able to take on new information and process thoughts, feelings, beliefs, and emotions. Don't worry, I won't go all 'sciencey' on you. If you want to understand how stress affects the body and brain in more detail, there are already many books and articles out there. All you have to do is google 'how stress affects my brain' and you'll have a full-time job, sorting through it all, right there.

I'd like to give you a brief overview of how our stress response affects the functioning of the mind and therefore, our ability to think clearly and process adequately.

Many of you will have heard of the 'fight, flight and freeze' response. This is our brilliant body's way of protecting us in the face of perceived danger. It's also referred to as our survival response. It's controlled by the autonomic nervous system (ANS). There are two parts of the ANS: the Sympathetic Nervous System (SNS) and the Parasympathetic Nervous System (PNS). The SNS turns on the stress response and the PNS restores the body to a state of calm. This can sometimes be hijacked, perceiving the innocuous as dangerous, particularly if stress is long-term.

When the body senses danger, either physical or psychological, the body shifts energy resources towards fighting or fleeing. The SNS signals the adrenal glands to release cortisol and adrenalin. This is where the physical sensations of stress come from. Essentially, your body requires the big muscles of your limbs to function at their optimum for survival and, at that moment, inhibits your digestive system and 'thinking' brain. This occurs because when there is real danger survival is paramount and thinking and digestion are redundant and only slow the process required for your survival.

This part of the brain acts automatically, below our conscious awareness, meaning we have no control over it. Think of it this way, our primitive brain evolved while our ancestors were in the jungle with the potential of being chased by a tiger. It often misinterprets modern day events, like your child coming out, as a danger to life, resulting in your thinking brain shutting down when you need it most. Therefore, it makes it difficult to sort through your thoughts and feelings, think clearly, make decisions, and remember appointments, among other things. It can also make us more emotional and if stress is high or sustained, numb.

Alison was likely under long-term stress which doesn't necessarily shut down the 'thinking' brain but compromises it over time. This is probably what she was experiencing and the extra stress of her child coming out tipped her over.

What do you need to reduce the overwhelm? You need your PNS to function effectively to help calm your system, so it can redistribute your energy sources to the required areas, particularly the frontal lobes, the thinking parts of the brain. How do you do this? We need to convince our unconscious brains the danger has dissipated. Please note, this won't happen immediately and will vary for every individual. If there has been stress for a long period, the brain becomes hypervigilant and will see danger where there isn't any, maintaining high levels of stress. There are a variety of strategies you can use to convince your brain the danger has gone. I have created a list to get you started. Take it one step at a time.

Begin by considering what brings you joy and add that to your own list. You can also try these suggestions:

- Breathing: - take a few minutes to focus on your breath. Allow it to slow and deepen. You can also try any of the breathing exercises I've shared in this book or any of the below strategies:

- Meditation

- Yoga

- Walk in nature (or anywhere if you're not near nature)

- Sit in your garden

- Focus on something beautiful, a flower, the ocean, a tree, a crystal etc (not a person)

- Listen to calming music

- Watch a comedy (laughing therapy is great)

- Read

- Draw, paint, colour in (or other forms of creativity)

- Play music

- Exercise - be mindful that you don't re-trigger the SNS (avoid overdoing it and avoid exercise that might stimulate the fight or flight response, e.g. boxing, hard running)

Other things to consider in your pursuit to reduce overwhelm.

- Put yourself first: - putting others first all the time doesn't make you a better parent or person. In fact, it often results in the opposite.

- Fill your cup first: - this doesn't equal neglecting loved ones. In fact, they need you to do it. It enables you to show up for your loved ones as the best you can be. You can't 'serve' others with an empty cup. Fill yours till it's overflowing and serve others the overflow in the saucer. Then you get the best of both worlds.

- Build your toolbox: - None of this is an 'either/or' scenario. The more you have in your toolbox, the more likely you are to have the exact right tool for the job. A builder doesn't just have one screwdriver, spanner, and hammer. They have several, so they're prepared for any job. Build it gradually, beginning with small, easy steps.

- Ask for what you need: - this can be tough for the 'giving types', however, it is important. Your loved ones are not mind readers. Refer to point one. It's also good role modelling for your children.

- Declutter your space: - a decluttered space equals a decluttered mind. Start with one small area at a time and note how it feels. It may take time, like building a wall, one brick at a time.

- Be kind to yourself: - avoid criticism, judgement and harsh language. No one likes to be told off, judged, or called horrible names, including you. Stop doing it to yourself. That's right. You're not an idiot, or stupid, so stop saying it. Even if you 'didn't really mean it'. We're listening and our own voices are the loudest. It does impact you. I know, easier said than done. Much of this self-talk is below conscious awareness, hence the helpfulness of practising mindfulness.

- Stop comparing your insides to others' outsides: - you don't know what others are feeling or thinking. We too often make assumptions from what we see on the outside and often we're wrong. Comparing is only hurting you.

- Access support for yourself: - be open to receive, and remember, asking for support does not equal an unsupportive parent. After years of working with young people, the most common thing I heard, from those whose parents accessed support, was how happy it made them. It sent a very clear message of love to them. They felt seen, heard, and understood. They knew their parents cared enough to invest in accessing support to become more informed. They were relieved that they didn't have to be the support or educator for their parents and that there was hope of returning to a 'normal' life.

A message from the parents of Rainbow Transformations

(Indigo Journey's private Facebook community. We'd love you to join us.)

The parents in my private Facebook community for parents of LGBTQ+ folk wanted to share a message with you all. Here's what they said:

- "Be compassionate towards yourself."

- "Work towards understanding the reasons for your

choices/behaviours/responses. Even if you've made mistakes, show yourself some kindness." (seeing our mistakes is the best form of learning)

- "Find gratitude for what you did and are doing well."

- "Keep perspective on what you're doing well, what you're learning and how you are working towards healing for you, your child and your relationship."

- "Forgive yourself and allow yourself time."

- "These feelings will pass. Give yourself some time and space to process your feelings."

- I'd like to leave you with this quote from Nelson Mandala

- "It *always seems impossible until it's done.*"

MOP ~ Trust your heart and your body

Safe Hold

Find a comfortable seat. Somewhere that feels safe and private, at least for a few minutes.

Place your left hand on your heart, and your right hand on your belly.

Take a nice deep breath in and as we did in Chapter 1, allow the exhale to guide your body to release any tension it's holding.

On the inhale, notice how your chest and belly expand. Feel the gentle pressure that creates against your hands. Repeat this 3 times. Imagine you're giving yourself a hug.

Allow your breath to return to its natural state.

Invite self-compassion to your heart and your belly, through your hands.

Repeat after me – This too will pass. I'm doing the best I can. It's ok to feel what I feel. I am not alone.

And again – This too will pass. I'm doing the best I can. It's ok to feel what I feel. I am not alone.

One more time – This too will pass. I'm doing the best I can. It's ok to feel what I feel. I am not alone.

Hold your hands there for as long as you need or want to.

When it's time to let your hands go, notice what you feel...

If it feels helpful, write it in your journal.

Let's Take Action ~ You've got this!

Find your choice for change

Begin by creating a bit of quiet time so your mind can focus. Put your phone away or turn the notifications off. Grab some paper and a few pens or markers. It helps to have a few different colours.

Start writing everything you feel is contributing to the over-whelm, without filtering. Leave nothing out. Include even the smallest of things, even things that initially feel silly. It all contributes. Once I think I've completed the list, I ask myself, "And what else?"

This is a very simple, but powerful trick that I learned from a good friend and colleague many years ago. The reason it's so effective is that our brain filters itself, sometimes without us knowing. It will leave out those things that it erroneously interprets as trivial, meaningless, embarrassing etc and that is often where the gold is. Continue the list and ask one more time, "And what else?" It's important to get it all written down.

Don't worry about being repetitive. Write, write, write. No filter, no analysis, judgement, criticism, or grammar police.

This is an exercise that can be repeated throughout the process to monitor progress and change.

Once you're satisfied your list is complete, create 3 categories.

1. I have full control, influence or say over it (orange)

2. I have partial control, influence or say over it (green)

3. I have no control, influence or say over it (blue).

In the next part, you're going to circle each one with the relevant colour. I've given you examples, however, you can choose your own.

Look at each individual item on your list and ask yourself:

"How much influence, control or say over it, do I have?" (don't automatically settle for the first answer. Always ask yourself, "Are you sure?" You can also take a break, as your brain will process while you're distracted)

- If the answer is 'no control', and you're sure – circle it in blue.

- If the answer is "yes, I have some control or influence", your next job is to determine how much. Complete control or influence – circle orange and partial – circle green.

- If the answer is, "I'm not sure", to any of your responses, simply ask again.

Be as honest with yourself as possible, because the more say you have, the more empowering it is. In the beginning, it might feel easier to externalise the blame or responsibility, however, in the long run, it isn't. Be kind to yourself. This is a process and I encourage you to seek a support person if you haven't already.

This exercise is to identify your choices. The more choices we have, the more empowered we feel. Of course, there may be some things that you honestly feel you have no control over. In this case, for now, I'd encourage you to focus your attention where you do have some control or influence.

The next step is deciding what to do with this information. Do you make different choices and work on changing your perspectives, or do you continue as things are? Whatever your decision is, it's okay. Knowing you have more options than you thought is more useful and will help ease at least a little of the overwhelm. It's sitting in your mind and you're getting used to the idea of change. I would strongly encourage aiming for tiny changes, rather than big changes in this initial stage. An accumulation of smaller successes will likely facilitate further change and help shut down that critical voice.

Deciding to do things differently can often be a difficult one and require some extra support. Don't let that put you off, seek the support you need and create the life and relationships you want and deserve. A friend of mine once said… "The act of identifying you need help and seeking it, is a sign of intelligence and courage." What a wise woman she is.

Key Points

- To be the best you can be, you must fill your own cup first

- Origins of overwhelm and expectations

- Psychology – how stress impacts our ability to function at our full potential

- How To Reduce 'The Overwhelm'

- You Can Offer Your Child Support While Asking for Support - They'll Love It

- Be Kind To Yourself - Reflect Without Judgment

Chapter 3

Parents Come Out Too

Navigating New Waters With Consent

"You're braver than you believe, stronger than you seem, and smarter than you think."

~ Winnie the Pooh ~

There's a lot of hype and discussion within and about the LGBTQ+ community about 'coming out'. It can be scary, daunting, overwhelming, and confusing for everyone. Your child has just taken this enormous step to share with you and now you have to consider the who's, how's and when's of this process yourself. You also have the added burden of, "Should I or shouldn't I?", "It's not my news to tell" and/or "Is it better for them if I do it for them?", just to name a few. Before we go into this in more detail, let's talk about what exactly 'coming out' means. It may seem obvious; however, I'll clarify so that we're on the same page.

What is coming out and how does it work?

Coming out is a term used to describe the process of an LGBTQ+ person sharing or opening up to someone about their sexuality and/or gender identity. However, as you might have realised, it's not just for the LGTBQ+ individual. Parents, siblings, grandparents, and other family members also have the consideration whether to come out in various situations.

Before we go any further, I want to share an alternative term with you that I like to use. Many years ago, the young people I worked with taught me this term. It is 'inviting in'. The reason I like this more is it feels more empowering and warmer, and it gives agency to the individual. I remember a young person sharing the purpose of using this alternative term. It was like a light bulb turned on, for me. It made so much sense. Here's what they shared with me.

"Coming out implies there is something bad about me that I have to work myself up to disclosing. That there's some kind of social obligation for me to disclose to the world." They continued, "Inviting in, feels more empowering. More like I have a say. I feel like this is an important, valid part of who I am that I can choose to share, if and when I'm ready. I can choose who, when and where to invite people into my world, to know more about me, when I feel ready. It no longer feels like a societal expectation or sharing something that is bad."

What are your thoughts about this?

It can also pertain to family members. Take a moment to consider the difference in your own experience. Think about a person you feel you need or want to 'come out' to. How are you feeling about it? Now think about the possibility of inviting that person in. How does that feel? Does it feel any different?

The alternate term is not for everyone and if it's not for you, that's ok. I alternate between the two, partly out of habit and partly because many people are not aware of the alternative. I encourage you to explore using this term, at least to yourself, when you're considering the possibility of sharing with others and see if it eases the burden at all. (or helps you to feel you have more agency)

'Coming out' or 'inviting others in' can bring up a lot of emotions and fear. What many people don't realise, and you might not realise either, is that this is not a one-off experience. It's not a single period in time where you decide to share this news about your child and once you've told those closest to you, it's all done. There is of course, the original person or people, you decide to tell, and then there may be a list of others who you want to share with, at some stage. But that's not where it stops. It continues throughout life, as you meet new people, go to new places, and have new experiences. It's obviously a lot more present for your child, however, you'll also experience the need to consider the sharing of this part of your child (loved one).

It's not just your child who comes out

As I just mentioned, and you've probably realised yourself, it's not just your child that has to come out, or at least consider whether they're going to, to whom and in what circumstances.

This is also a big part of your journey. The difference is you can't simply make your own decisions. You must consider and consult your child in each of those decisions you make.

As time goes by, the process may become less consultative, however, the golden rule is:

"It's never okay to come out, about someone else, without their explicit consent."

This means that regardless of how you're feeling, you need to consult your child before you share with anyone. That includes your partner, your parents, their siblings, your best friend, anyone. It's also important that you don't coerce/encourage your child to come out to any particular person. You can have an open discussion, however, be mindful that you are not coercing them. This can be a tricky line to walk, but once you've shared the news, you can't take it back and they're ultimately the ones that have to live with the other person's reactions and responses.

That being said, I want to acknowledge and explore the difficulty for you in making these decisions and having these conversations, even with your child's consent. It can be daunting to share information with others when you're uncertain of how they'll respond, particularly if you're still struggling. Even if you're confident they'll be ok, it can be scary. There are so many things to consider, and they can exacerbate the struggles because the decision to share this news is not solely yours.

In the past, you may have shared some things about your child, with your partner, friend, or parent, without their consent and that may have been okay in those circumstances. Now you know you can't do that in this situation it may be hard to figure out what's ok and therefore feel difficult to access support. You may feel you just need someone to talk to. Send me an email to request a copy of your free Guide For Parents of LGBTQ+ Kids - How to Find Support.

Your struggles

Let's explore your struggles. How are you feeling about sharing the news about your child? I'm sure this varies depending on who you're considering telling, however, there will be some similar apprehensions. Like your child, some of these will be conscious and others less conscious. You'll be assessing for safety, judgement, and/or rejection. Scanning for signs of openness and acceptance. Asking yourself questions like, "What will they think? Will they judge me or my child?" Or "Will they be rude, abusive or dismissive?" Will they continue to love and support you and your child in the same way? Will it affect your relationships with friends, colleagues, and other family members? Will they look at you differently, speak to you differently, or treat you differently? Will they ask questions you don't know how or are uncomfortable answering?

There are many things to think about, and if you're still strug-gling to come to terms with your child's sexuality or gender identity, this will be more difficult. It can exacerbate your feelings of fear, uncertainty, confusion, and worry, making it feel impossible to even consider what, when, who and how.

So, what next?

Stop and take a few breaths. Remember our MOPs at the end of each chapter. Now is a good time to practice one of those.

Understand, you don't need to do it right away. Just the same as your child, no one can decide to come out for you, except for your child, if they have requested you share it with someone for them. If this is the case, have a conversation with your child about whether it is crucial you do it right away and exactly what they want you to share. You can also ask them for a bit of time to process yourself before you do it.

Strategies to consider

There are some strategies I support parents and LGBTQ+ people to use as part of the 'inviting in' process below. You can use this as a guide for yourself and to offer to your child and other family members.

- Discuss with your child first (remember the golden rule) and make sure you're clear on what they want to be shared and with who. You also don't need to take on this responsibility for them, depending on their age.

- Assess for safety: - emotional and physical.

- Do it in your own time: - if you have your child's explicit consent, it's then up to you, when you feel ready and able to share.

- Work through your own feelings first: - it's a good idea to give yourself some time and space to process before you tell too many people. It's best, to begin with one or two people who can be supportive.

- Build your allies: - choose people that you're most confident will be an ally and leave the more challenging people for later.

- Dip your toe in the water: - touch on an LGBTQ+ topic that's currently in the media to get a sense of the person's attitude. Keep in mind their response about a stranger will not always be the same as their response about a loved one.

- Consider your timing: - choose a time when you won't be distracted, you have the time, without one of you needing to rush off and consider each of your stress levels. It's much harder to take in new information when stressed by other things.

When you're ready

Remember, there's no pressure for you to come out unless it is a need or desire of your child. If this is the case, you may have less say, and this is something that I work through with my clients, often. We talk through their feelings, their child's feelings, how to communicate with their child, whether there can be a compromise and how to best manage the situation for everyone's benefit. Remember, not everyone needs to know straight away. In fact, not everyone needs to know.

If it is not a need or desire for your child, then you can do it in your own time. It is important to note that being reluctant to share this news about your child can, over time, feel for your child, like you're ashamed or embarrassed. Therefore, while I wholeheartedly support you to do it in your own time, it is important to be actively working towards this goal. Sitting idle and avoiding it will only increase the risk of your child experiencing increased feelings of shame, isolation and rejection.

What does this mean? Continue to take action, move towards being able to share, and communicate openly with your child. Ensure they know it is about your processing and understanding, rather than how you feel about them.

Things to consider

Invite them in? Or don't invite them in?

As we've discussed there are an array of things for you to consider when deciding whether to come out and tell others about your child's identity (or journey?), these include:

- Do you have explicit consent from your child?

- Are you comfortable enough?

- Who does it, who decides this?

- Who should be informed?

- When will you do it?

- How will you do it?

- Why do it at all?

- Not always necessary.

Explicit consent

As mentioned above, it is crucial you have explicit consent from your child before you tell anyone. If the answer is yes from them, you can skip to the 'Are you comfortable' section below, if it's no or not yet, let's explore that further. There are an array of reasons your child may not want to come out to the person you are thinking of. They may be clear about the reason/s or they may not. Regardless, it is important for you to respect their decision. Sometimes this may be easy enough and other times it might be challenging, regardless, you must respect your child's wishes.

If it is someone that you were hoping to get support from, or a significant person in your life it may feel uncomfortable keeping a secret from them. This could become more difficult over time. In these circumstances, it is worth having a conversation with your child to better understand their reluctance and support, not coerce, them through it.

Reassure them you're not trying to convince them, rather you want to better understand so you can support them and perhaps eventually get to a place where they are comfortable. Practice active, non-defensive listening (we talk more about this in Chapter 8). Acknowledge your child's point of view. Ask them if it is ok for you to share your reasons for wanting to share their news so that together you might find a solution. Respect their choice if they're not able to hear you at this point. (If this is the case find someone you can talk with while respecting their wishes) Your child can't stop you from talking to a therapist, counsellor, or coach. These professionals are bound by confidentiality ethics, values, and laws, therefore, regardless of how your child is feeling, it's safe to discuss your feelings with one of them.

One of the biggest dilemmas for parents is when their child doesn't want their parent's partner to know. Unfortunately, as difficult as this may be for you, it is important for you to respect their wishes and even more important to reach out for some professional support. There are many reasons your child may be reluctant for your partner to know, whether or not they're the other parent, and the golden rule still stands. Your child may feel uncomfortable, unsafe, or simply unsure of how your partner may respond. You may feel like those feelings are not warranted, however as mentioned, once you've shared the news, it can't be taken back. Unfortunately, my experience has shown me that people often react differently than expected, therefore regardless of how you think your partner will react you must respect your child's wishes. You might find it helpful to reach out for professional support to develop strategies to manage the challenges that arise, as a result.

In some families, it can become an uncomfortable, unsafe, and often abusive environment for LGBTQ+ people and/or the supportive parent. This is sometimes completely unexpected and one reason it's important not to 'out' your child against their wishes. In these circumstances, it is vital that the supportive parent prioritise their child's and their own safety (regardless of their age) and reach out for support and guidance.

As mentioned, you can never guarantee how an individual will respond, even your partner, so there needs to be time for your child to feel ok, for them to feel safe and comfortable. There may be some things you can do, subtly, but be mindful this is a fine line to walk. Remember, they have trusted you with this information and they need to know they can continue to trust you.

Jackie

When I met Jackie, she was beside herself. Her son had just come out as bisexual and had made her promise not to tell her partner, his dad. This felt extremely uncomfortable for Jackie. She and her husband didn't keep secrets from each other. They prided themselves in parenting as a team and it felt like a betrayal to keep this from him. Something inside her said she had to listen to her child, even though it felt so uncomfortable.

Jackie later shared with me that her hope was, when she came to see me, that I would "make it ok" for her to share with him. As you could guess, I didn't. What I did was support Jackie through her own feelings and thoughts, both about her son being bi and the expectation that she keep it from her husband. Of course, this is a difficult situation, however, as I mentioned earlier, it is important that Jackie not betray her child's trust. We did some work around her being able to support her son to feel safer to open up to his dad and to be less worried about disappointing him. When Jackie could understand her son's concerns more deeply, she was more able to support him through his own process to trust that his dad loved him enough for this not to cause a problem.

Jackie also created subtle conversations with her husband to ensure he was going to respond appropriately.

When the day came, Jackie's son was able to invite his dad in, himself, with Jackie's support. This experience, while difficult, was an incredible opportunity for the whole family to deepen their connections with each other. Jackie learned more about her son, they became much closer; he learned he could depend on his Mum 100%, even if she was put in a difficult position with her own husband. Her son and husband also deepened their bond through this process.

Jackie's husband was upset when he first heard that she had known for some time before him and that she hadn't told him, however, once he understood the situation, he could appreciate that his son was able to talk with him, himself. This was possible because Jackie and her son, through their communication with each other, had both deepened their own understanding and therefore able to share that with him.

There's no denying it is tough to keep secrets from your significant other, or other loved ones. Please remember that it is your child who is the most vulnerable in this situation, as is your relationship with them. It's crucial to keep their trust and buy some time to work this through. If this is the situation you're in, I strongly encourage you to get support where you can and remember it is (usually) only a temporary situation.

If you are reading this after you've come out about your child, without their consent, don't worry. Don't give yourself a hard time. That won't benefit anyone. If appropriate, apologise to your child. Let them know that you now know better and ask them what you can do to repair any damage that may have been done. They'll most likely appreciate you for doing the work to learn how to best support them and have more understanding of your mistakes. Be mindful not to have expectations about how they should respond. If they're hurt, it may take some time to forgive. Hot tip: don't make a big fuss, because that just gets awkward for everyone and puts them in a position to feel like they have to make you feel better.

Maya Angelou says it best:

"Do the best you can until you know better. Then when you know better, do better."

Comfortable enough

You don't have to invite anyone in until it feels okay. As long as you have your child's consent, you can make the choice in your own time, when you feel ready. The more comfortable you're feeling about your child's sexuality and/or gender identity, the easier it will feel. And of course, the less comfortable you feel the more uncomfortable and challenging it will be. Being uncomfortable doesn't mean don't do it, as like anything new, it will carry a level of discomfort, at least in the beginning. Keep in mind telling someone who you think will help you process this information and become more comfortable might be helpful.

I encourage you to put aside any expectations or beliefs you have, that xxx (insert family or friend) deserves to be told, or we really should tell xxx (insert family or friend) before we tell xxx (insert family or friend). This only makes a tough situation tougher. Get more comfortable yourself, before inviting any-one else in. I encourage you to follow my suggestions above, even though it might feel different to how you usually decide about sharing important information.

Another thing to consider is whether you are the person do-ing the sharing or it is your child, with your support. We've touched on this earlier and the answer is always, it's up to your child, first and foremost. They may want to be the one, or they might ask for your or someone else's help. If they're asking for your help, ensure you're clear on the details.

For example, a family I worked with recently shared that their child wanted their parents to share with the broader family, however, didn't want them to share any details yet. This felt difficult for the parents as it meant they couldn't answer questions the family might have. They needed to talk through the details with their child so they could get a better understanding of what their child wanted and their reasons for not wanting details shared. There were some compromises made that felt in line with the child's wishes and also made the conversations feel more approachable for the parents. The child also suggested sending the information in a text mes-sage, except for the grandparents. The message was to include the fact that they couldn't answer questions, at this point, out of respect for their child. This made it much easier than a face-to-face discussion, with the awkwardness of refusing to answer the inevitable questions.

Open communication can usually find the answers. During these conversations it's important to clarify with your child who they're comfortable with you telling and whether they mind when and how you do it. If they're open, these are questions for you to answer for yourself, remembering there is no rush, go at your own pace. A good question to ask yourself is why you're considering sharing at all because you don't have to. It is not everyone's business. Often parents feel like they have to make an announcement to everyone, however, it's important to think through the purpose of telling people and ask yourself if it's necessary. You don't have an obligation to anyone. No one is entitled to this information. Below are some examples of when it's necessary or not.

A colleague that you talk to occasionally in the lunchroom vs a colleague that you eat lunch with every day and talk about your family. Your best friend from school who you see twice a year, vs your current best friend. A cousin that moved abroad that you haven't seen for three years vs a close cousin you see at least once a month.

In all these examples there is no need to go out of your way to share about your child, however, you might decide to share with the second person in each scenario for support. There's no reason not to tell the first person, but that might happen down the track if it comes up in conversation. This is all about reducing the overwhelm. Ask yourself do you need to tell them and why. Perhaps the answer is yes, but not now. The key is to give yourself space to process your own feelings first.

Jason

I once worked with a father, Jason, who found it very difficult, when his child first came out and was highly anxious about his work colleagues finding out he had an LGBTQ+ son. Jason has come a long way since we met, because he's done a lot of work to process his feelings, he's been able to gain the confidence to share the news with a couple of his friends. This eventually led to him feeling more able to share with some colleagues.

From past conversations he'd witnessed and the general culture, in the workplace, he felt like it was a homophobic and transphobic environment. He was worried about his opportunities for promotion being affected, his relationships with colleagues, and how they would look at him and treat him. Even more concerning for him was that he was unsure how he would manage if someone said something horrible about his child. He wasn't confident he could remain professional.

We spent some time exploring his options. Option one, say nothing to anyone. Option two, tell everyone everything immediately. Option three, four, five, six, is anything in between! He realised that it was not actually the business of anyone at work, so there was no real rush to tell them. He could tolerate the awkward conversations a little longer while he planned his approach. It was great that he was already thinking about it, because as he said, "it was likely to come up again at some stage, and it was better to be prepared." So, prepared is exactly what he became. Find out what steps Jason took in chapter 9.

MOP ~ Trust your heart and your body

Box Breath

We'll take a few moments to connect to your breath. You'll notice that we'll explore a variety of breathing exercises, as this creates a wonderful opportunity to connect with your body and calm your nervous system. You may find that one works better for you, or you might like to keep them all in your toolbox. Remember to always listen to your body. If something doesn't feel right for you, try something else.

Box breath is a lovely breathing exercise used to calm the system, clear the mind and connect to your body. It can also be helpful if you're having trouble sleeping. It is a simple count of your breath - inhale for the count of four, hold your breath for four, exhale for four and hold for four. When you first start out, four might feel like a bit much, or if you're an experienced breather, you may feel more comfortable extending it out. The important element is that each action is for the same amount of time. Listen to your body and respond accordingly. It is common for people to struggle more with either of the holds. Be mindful that you don't want to be straining, so if that's you, reduce your count to three until you feel more comfortable.

If you haven't already, find yourself a comfortable seat. Begin by noticing your breath, without adjusting it, simply notice. Where do you feel it most? The nostrils, the top lip, the throat, chest or belly? This is a great way to begin any relaxation or breathing exercise.

Begin Box Breath:

- Inhale for four

- Hold for four

- Exhale for four

- Hold for four

Continue for a minimum of four rounds. You can, of course, do more and if you feel a little lightheaded, simply return to your natural breath for a few breaths and then you can continue when it feels right for you.

Notice what you feel...

If it feels helpful, write it in your journal.

Take Action ~ You've got this!

Dress Rehearsal

If there's someone important you want to tell and you're nervous, create a plan and practice writing them a letter. I've done this many times with young people wanting to come out to their parents. You don't have to follow through with the plan exactly, however, the process is helpful to reduce the worry and stress.

Write your responses to the following questions:

- When might be a good time and what are times to avoid?

- What's important when you tell them, for example, is it important for someone else to be there? Is there time for discussion afterwards? Do they have other stressors happening? Perhaps not when they're driving a car!

- What are the important points you want to make?

- Will they need an explanation or more information? Ensure you have this information.

Write a practice letter. You can read this to them, send it to them, or use it as a 'prompt card'. Or you might just use it as a processing tool for you. If you give it to them, you might wait around for them to read it or leave a note at the bottom with instructions for them to call you when they've read it.

Young people and other parents have found this process extremely helpful as a tool to work through what they want to communicate and to get more comfortable. Some even practice reading their letter out loud. You might also have your own ideas. The key element is to ease or at least process some of your worries, fears and discomfort.

Key Points

- Inviting In vs Coming Out

- Your Child's Consent Comes First

- Keep Communication Open with Your Child

- Setting Up Boundaries for You and Your Child

- In Your Own Time and Your Own Way

- It's Not Always Necessary to Share

Chapter 4

Beliefs And Values

Untangling What Belongs To You

"Keep my word positive. Words become my behaviors. Keep my behaviors positive. Behaviors become my habits. Keep my habits positive. Habits become my values. Keep my values positive. Values become my destiny."

~ Mahatma Gandhi ~

Beliefs and values – how they affect you and those around you

First, I want to be clear. I will not try to change your values or beliefs. This is not and will never be my aim. We are all entitled to our beliefs and values. What we're not entitled to, is to use those to cause harm to others, intentionally or unintentionally. I am under no illusion, and neither should you be. This chapter has the potential to be challenging and possibly confronting, however, it's important, very important, if you're to have a healthy relationship with your LGBTQ+ child. It's vital to your well-being and the health, safety and well-being of your child to explore and deepen your understanding of your beliefs and values, how they affect your thoughts and feelings and, therefore, your behaviours, responses and reactions.

The aim of this chapter is to raise your awareness and understanding of how our beliefs and values might affect our understanding of our children and, therefore, our behaviour. Research findings show the critical role of family acceptance and rejection on LGBTQ+ folk (Ryan & Diaz, 2011; Ryan & Chen-Hayes, 2013). This means you can make a significant difference in your child's well-being by doing some work to better understand your feelings, thoughts, and emotions. Deepening your understanding of where your beliefs and values come from and if they still feel right, help to make meaning for you. Doing this work will put you in a position to create a safe, supportive, loving, and inclusive family space for your child to thrive.

What are your values and beliefs about sexuality and gender identity? When I asked myself this question, many years ago, I was shocked at how hard I found it to answer. It was not something I'd spent a lot of time consciously thinking about. I had subconsciously accepted the hetero-normative narrative I'd been exposed to my whole life. I'd explored gender from a feminist perspective, however, even though I challenged a lot of binary beliefs about gender, my default perspective took me right back to the common messaging from society. Any area I pushed outside of the common belief systems, I judged as being something wrong with me or bad.

Be kind to yourself and allow some time to reflect on what your beliefs and values are. Some will be obvious and others more subtle. It's often the subtle ones that catch us off guard and impact our behaviour without us realising. *Because these are so ingrained from an early age, it is likely that you will find this particularly challenging to do on your own. I encourage you to reach out to someone (preferably a professional) to support you through this process.*

Are they yours?

Before we explore some common beliefs and values, it's good to think about where they come from and who they actually belong to. We don't just make them up on our 7th birthday. They're not something we're born with. We gather our beliefs and values from a variety of sources along this wonderful journey called life. A large portion will come from our parents or primary caregivers. As we grow and are exposed to more people and greater social input, the sources of our beliefs and values can become more entrenched. In saying that, our parents lay the foundations, through their own input and their influence over the people and environments we're exposed to. The friends we visit, the family we spend time with, the place of worship we attend, the school we attend, the media and the hobbies and other interests we're involved in.

All of this occurs as our brains are developing. Before the 'decision-making' part of our brain is fully developed. Therefore, our values and beliefs have been handed down by our parents and other significant adults in our lives. As they feel familiar and normal to us, we rarely question them, explore them, or look at them with curiosity. We assume they're our own. When in truth, we have inherited them. Like other things we inherit, we may be perfectly happy with them, and perhaps there are some that we don't need to continue to carry. The important part is to explore them with an open, curious mind and decide for yourself.

PAUSE

The activity at the end of this chapter guides you through this process, so I'm going to invite you to pause your reading and jump to the end of this chapter and start this activity. It will allow you some extra personal insight as you read on...

...Great, now you've got your list, let's keep reading. Keeping in mind you can adjust your list any time you need to.

Religion and Culture

Let's begin with what is possibly, for many people, two of the most powerful influences and therefore the most challenging to shift. Religion and culture. I know these two things are not the same, however, they're also often closely connected. We won't go into depth here, as we couldn't possibly do it justice in such a brief space, because there are many cultures and religions and, of course, a variety of beliefs and values within each.

Religion and culture are often very close to an individual's heart and identity. Your community and friendships may be centred around your faith and/or culture. They can influence your whole sense of being and belonging. This makes it extremely difficult if either or both are not accepting of your child's sexuality or gender identity.

It can feel like you're being made to choose between your child and your own identity and community. You may even feel like your child has a choice about their gender identity or sexual orientation and is doing this just to spite you or challenge you. I want to reassure you that this is not the case. This is how your child is feeling. They're not trying to hurt you or make life difficult. They need your love and support. If you have brought them up with similar faith, beliefs, and/or culture, they will probably have very similar struggles and fears as you.

I know that reading these words in this book will not change what you believe automatically, nor is it asking you to. The process of unpacking and understanding will definitely take time. So, what can you do in the meantime? What will change things? What will bring peace to your mind and heart?

Take a moment to reconnect with your child in your heart. Using your imagination and memories, regardless of their age, remember that beautiful baby you brought home, the little toddler that raced around your home bringing loads of laughs, tears, fears and joy. Can you feel how that felt? Remember the moment you found out you were going to be a parent? You likely said something like, I don't care what gender my child is, as long as they are healthy and happy. Do you remember that feeling? Take a moment to bring yourself back to that time, feel what you felt, and connect your heart to that little person you brought into your family.

Regardless of the news your child has shared with you, they're still the same person. Connect to that. Hold on to that. This is crucial, to allow you the time and space you need to reconcile your faith and cultural beliefs with your feelings for your child. This will take time, so it's important to stay connected with your child. It's also okay to grieve or feel any other emotions you're feeling.

I understand that this can be easier said than done. If your and your family's religious and cultural beliefs conflict with your child's identity, this can bring up some big emotions for everyone. Be mindful, kind, and compassionate to yourself and your child. Keep in mind, now is not the time to reinforce those beliefs with your child, even though you might have the urge to do so. They already know. It has taken them a lot of courage to share this with you. They'll have their own struggles they're trying to work through. If that urge feels too strong to resist, perhaps you can write what you're wanting to say, as a strategy to express your feelings, without sharing them with your child. It's amazing how helpful this process can be.

Seek support to process this for yourself. Find an unbiased person who can support you. In difficult times, you may be used to turning to your community leaders, however, if they have a closed or one-sided view on this topic that may not feel like the safest or most beneficial option. They are unlikely to be able to support you to explore all sides. The same as talking to someone who is opposed to your religious or cultural beliefs also won't be able to. Finding a neutral person might feel challenging, however, it is important.

Minimise your discussions about your child with others who are opposed or not understanding, for now. Find yourself support who can hear your pain, your struggles and your fears without judgement and without feeding them. You need someone who can create a safe, supportive space for you to explore your feelings (ALL of them) and make your decisions.

Gender identity, expression, roles, and expectations

Gender roles are another area that is deeply ingrained in us from a very young age. It is common to have a binary, rigid approach to expectations around gender identity, expression, and roles. These expectations will stem from a variety of areas in your life and often remain unquestioned or explored. Religion and culture can have a significant impact on our beliefs and expectations around gender expression and roles, however, stereotypes and societal expectations about gender have always shifted and changed. Lots of things influence this, politics, societal expectations, women's rights movements... etc.

In many areas of the world, gender roles and expectations have shifted over the years. Some would say, not enough and I'm sure there are some that say too much. Regardless of your thoughts on that, the fact remains that we have many ideas and expectations about gender and we're not always conscious of them. Often stereotypes fuel these, either going 'with' them or 'against' them.

Think, for example, about how clothing styles have changed. In the 1800s, it would have been unthinkable for a woman to wear trousers or pants, but by the 1930s and 40s, this had changed significantly. Think about the fact that only 40 years ago, when a woman got married, she was expected to quit her job so she could stay at home and keep a clean house and have children. We've taken a further step in this area, in recent years, where in some jobs, men can receive paid parental leave after the birth of their child. It's also becoming more common for couples to choose for the mother to return to work, while the father stays home to care for the child and home.

Despite my last point, even in today's most liberal of families, there can be an underlying expectation that the 'man' of the house takes care of the family financially. That they need to be stoic and, therefore, when they show emotions, it can feel difficult, uncomfortable and sometimes disconcerting. I've worked with many men who've felt the burden of this, even though they and their partner considered themselves quite liberal and proactively challenged those ideals within their family. One man shared with me, "I just can't seem to shake it. I know we're both equal, and she's an intelligent, capable, skilled doctor. There is no need for me to carry this burden, yet I do." He was completely unaware of the underlying expectations he was carrying until we spent some time exploring what his struggles truly were. To say they shocked him is an understatement.

Your beliefs and values around gender roles and expectations can have a significant impact on your understanding of your child and their gender or sexuality. They may be obvious or more subtle, like the guy I mentioned above. You may be unintentionally perpetuating gender stereotypes or expectations that affect your ability to see and hear your child, like Josie was.

More about Josie

Remember Josie from chapter one? She had missed opportunities to support her son when he was younger because of her underlying beliefs about gender roles and expectations. And then she continued to question and punish herself after he eventually shared with her he was gay. She had assumed that men who fall into the category of 'blokey' or masculine, are all straight. She had unconsciously connected his behaviours, interests and taste in clothing, cars, and furniture to being a heterosexual man. Upon reflection, she realised she had missed hints he had given her through his teenage years. She had dismissed his attempts to 'plant the seed' with her because she believed that only effeminate men were gay. She had an unconscious belief system that prevented her from seeing and hearing her son when he attempted to share his sexuality with her. This caused him to shut down, keep it to himself and eventually move far away from home, so he no longer had to hide that side of himself in his day-to-day life.

The story he told himself about that was that his mum wouldn't approve. That she wouldn't love him the same. She might even disown him. He now knows this isn't true. Josie struggled for a long time, punishing herself for not being there for him. It wasn't until she could recognise those deep beliefs and assumptions and the impact they had on how she saw the world that she could begin letting go of that guilt. We all make assumptions based on conscious and unconscious beliefs. The trick is to become more aware of them, so it's harder for them to sneak up behind us and have such an impact on our lives.

Cassie and Brody

Assumptions and beliefs about gender roles and expression impact people in a multitude of ways. For example, it inhibited Cassie, a parent I worked with a few years ago, from being able to continue supporting her 15-year-old trans child, Brody. Cassie hadn't realised she had quite traditional beliefs about gender. She unconsciously leaned towards the stereotypes of what girls and boys liked to play with, wear, and do. This realisation shocked her, as she had believed herself to be quite open and liberal. She had always encouraged her daughter to pursue any career she wished, she, semi reluctantly allowed her to cut her hair short and accepted that she was uncomfortable wearing dresses, so let go of her own desire to see her daughter in dresses, on special occasions.

When Cassie first came to see me and explained what was happening, she shared, "My daughter says she's a boy and I'm doing my best to accept this and do what she asks, but she still gets mad at me. I don't know what else to do." Cassie felt like she was being supportive by allowing Brody to do what they needed to do to affirm their gender. I later discovered, from Brody's perspective, there was a struggle at every turn. When Brody shared this with her, Cassie could justify it all in her mind, because "it's normal for a Mum to be sad when her daughter cuts her long hair off" and "I've always encouraged her to pursue whatever career she wants, even men's professions".

After a period of time, Cassie was able to realise that what Brody was upset about was that she continued to use the incorrect pronouns (which we'll talk about later), she was using language that reinforced gender stereotypes, without realising it (men's jobs, short hair, permission not to wear dresses), and she was putting up a fight before she agreed to anything, therefore Brody felt the need to fight back. While all of this is common and part of the process of Cassie figuring things out, it was frustrating for Brody and confusing for Cassie.

The confusion returned for Cassie, about 8 months later, when Brody shared they were perhaps not a boy, but also not a girl. Brody shared, "The best way I can describe how I feel is non-binary". They requested Cassie use they/them pronouns. Brody started wearing what you might describe as more feminine clothing and accessories every so often. They also wanted to go back to dance, however, chose hip-hop over ballet. Brody's interests, gender identity and expression were shifting, and this was difficult for Cassie.

After several months of not seeing Cassie, she returned to see me, as she knew from experience, when she was struggling, it affected Brody, regardless of how hard she tried to hide it. "I just don't get it", she shared. "If they want to wear feminine stuff occasionally and want to continue to dance, they keep hanging out with their girlfriends, why can't they just be a girl? Maybe they're a tomboy?"

These are all fair points, and Cassie is not alone in her confusion. The most helpful way to approach it is to understand that taste in clothing and interests don't determine a person's gender identity. Clothing and activities don't have a gender. We, as a society, put the gendered lens on particular colours, types of clothing, interests and behaviours, etc. For Brody, they'd let go of the need to prove their gender identity to be a particular way, because things at home had relaxed and that gave them the space to explore themselves more freely. While this was challenging and confusing for Cassie, it was an incredible gift she'd given her child because of the work she'd done previously. Brody was now feeling like they could take part in the activities they liked and express themselves in ways that felt most comfortable and authentic to them. This was a minor setback for Cassie and after working together for a little while longer, she felt more confident, comfortable, and connected to Brody than ever.

Another example is Australian rules football. Society originally considered it a male sport and that included spectators. Gradually women became more interested in watching the game (or it became more accessible for them to watch), and this increased over time, to where the gender split between spectators is now fairly even. For many years, girls wanted to play Aussie rules, however, this was not permitted. Over the years, girls' participation has increased, beginning with a kick around in the backyard or parks, to schoolyard participation and then fast forward to 2017, when the first season of AFLW (Australian Football League Women's) began. The national Australian Rules Football League for Women began with 8 teams and in 2022 was thriving with 18 teams.

Despite this significant shift over the last few years, I remember talking with a parent of a trans girl a couple of years ago and he said to me, "But she still wants to play football and go to games, so maybe she is still a boy."

In both these cases, the parents were being influenced by their unconscious beliefs, values, and biases around gender, and in varying degrees, it was causing more pain for them and their families and increased difficulty in supporting their children.

Marriage

Many of us have deep seated values and beliefs about marriage. What it should look like, who can get married, when is the right time, how the wedding should be, how to behave, what age it should happen, how long a couple should wait, etc. Many of these beliefs and values sit in the unconscious mind and are not brought to our awareness until something challenges them. This might be a couple announcing their wedding date earlier than believed appropriate, or them taking 'too long' to commit, maybe a pregnancy occurs before a wedding announcement, wedding plans are different to what's expected or a same-sex couple announcing their engagement.

In many countries, it is still illegal for same-sex couples to marry. Even in countries where it is legal, it's still quite recent and therefore not necessarily accepted or celebrated the same as a heterosexual wedding. Marriage is one of those things that parents often imagine and/or hope to happen for their children. The level of conscious awareness of these dreams varies, however, it's one of the most common concerns I hear from parents after their child comes out. They worry about them not getting married, and if they do, what that wedding will now look like. For those parents who don't accept the idea of a marriage, unless it is between a man and a woman that becomes even more of a challenge.

Peter and Shelly

Take Peter, for example. His 32-year-old gay daughter, Shelly, came out when she was 16. He thought he'd worked through his feelings and was 'ok' with her being gay. He thought he'd come to terms with the fact that her life might not look like he had envisaged, that she may not have kids and she wouldn't get married, as it wasn't legal at the time that she came out. When Shelly shared, her partner had proposed to her and they were planning on having a baby, Peter's reaction was a surprise to both of them.

When Peter arrived at our first appointment, I could see the fear on his face, the weight he was carrying on his shoulders. He found it very difficult to articulate what he was feeling, what his struggles were, and what they were about. Each time he began explaining his pain and his struggles, he stammered and followed quickly with, "But I already resolved this, years ago. I don't understand why I'm finding this so difficult. She's been with her girlfriend for years. I like her. They're both very happy. Why is this so hard?"

Peter shared that when his daughter first came out, in her teens, the most difficult thing for him was that she wouldn't get married and he wouldn't become a grandfather. He and his wife had talked it through and come to the realisation that this may not have happened, regardless of her sexuality, therefore they continued to love and support her and wait and see what the future brought. After all, they didn't want her to get married or have kids at 16, so there was still time.

When Shelly shared this news with Peter and his wife, he felt his stomach drop, his heart rate increase and his mind begin to spin. He couldn't pinpoint what that was all about, but he did his best to act like he was happy for her. He could see his wife was ecstatic. She appeared genuinely happy for their daughter and her long-time partner. He couldn't understand why he didn't feel the same.

When Peter and his wife were alone, he asked her how she felt. She was over the moon. In fact, she was so excited that she hadn't noticed his struggle. He was reluctant to share with her, as he felt embarrassed and ashamed of his internal struggle.

It made no sense. One of his dreams for his daughter was coming true. His baby girl was getting married and having a baby. He was going to be a grandad. This is what he wanted for her and for himself and his family. So why was he struggling so much?

Over several sessions, Peter worked through his feelings, his beliefs, how he saw the world and his thoughts about his gay daughter getting married and becoming a mother. He also explored what external influences affected the way he felt and how his own childhood had shaped his ideals around family. This process enabled him to become more aware of the real problem. The thing he was actually struggling with.

There were two key elements.

He realised that he was attached to the image he had in his head about his baby girl's wedding, and, he was worried that her baby wouldn't feel like his 'real' grandchild, as Shelly's partner was going to be the carrying mother.

Once this came to light, he was able to work through those feelings and come back to what was most important to him. His daughter's happiness. As with Josie, once he could calm his nervous system enough, by ceasing the judgement, criticism, shame and embarrassment. He could let go of those rigid ideals of what he had unknowingly hung on to since his daughter was born. Peter no longer felt the need to justify or defend himself, leaving more space to enjoy reality. He now understood that even though he didn't want to stay in that space or share those feelings with his daughter, they were still valid.

Even better, he was able to truly celebrate their news and play an active role in the wedding preparations, the conversations around the conception of their baby, the progress of the pregnancy and, of course, the life of his grandchild once they came along.

I saw Peter a couple of years after we completed our work together, and he was excited to share wedding and baby photos with me. In addition, he wanted to share a big revelation that he had several months after we had worked together. While he was enjoying all the celebration preparations, he was spending a lot more time with his daughter and partner and what he realised was that he was truly connecting with them both for the first time since Shelly came out, 16 years ago.

Due to the lack of authentically processing his feelings, 16 years ago, he was keeping his daughter at arm's length and hadn't gotten to know her partner at all. This was a simple strategy to protect himself from having to confront his true feelings. He was unconsciously afraid that if he allowed them the time and space, he might not feel the same love for his daughter, so he was in denial. He also didn't want to cause problems in his relationship with his wife. She appeared to fully support Shelly, and it embarrassed him to share exactly how he felt. He was extremely grateful for the opportunity to work through them in a safe, supportive environment, resulting in the development of a beautiful relationship with his daughter and her new little family.

Contemplation...

What are your beliefs and values about marriage? How did you envisage your child's future, in relation to marriage and relationships? Were you even conscious of those dreams or pictures you had? How are they affecting you now?

Family – what is it?

What does family mean to you? We all have ideas about what an ideal family looks like. What is that for you? There are many types of families in the world today, and they all have the potential to be wonderful and not so wonderful. This is not dependent on the gender or sexuality of its members, how many adults there are or how many people are in the family. I think most of us understand this on a cognitive level. However, when we have underlying beliefs or values that contradict each other, they can sneak up behind us and affect our thoughts and behaviours without us realising.

You also likely had some conscious or unconscious expectations about how your family might expand when your child grew up. This could be in the context of imagining their wedding, who they marry, and how their life will look. It may also be in the context of grandkids. How many you might have and the role you'll play in their lives? What kind of grandparent did you hope to be?

This might state the obvious, but none of this is guaranteed, regardless of your child's gender or sexuality. Depending on what country you live in and the desires of your child, neither of these are ruled out these days. Be aware that although you know this, on an intellectual level, you may still have some underlying fears or concerns. If so, it's worth exploring this further in a safe, supportive environment.

You may also have some family values or traditions that are creating an underlying discomfort for you in relation to your child's sexuality or gender identity. I remember one family I worked with had a particular tradition around marriage, for all the girls in the family. When their daughter came out as gay, it devastated her mother, as she thought it meant they were going to be breaking the family tradition.

After a considerable amount of reflection and exploration, she came to the realisation that she was not attached to the tradition. In fact, it felt outdated and forced. She could remember back to when she was planning her own wedding day and realised that she resented the expectation that she continue on the tradition that was created several generations ago. It restricted her own desires for her special day.

After this realisation, she went to the oldest living female relative and discussed the tradition, and how it affected her and her concerns and how it might affect her daughters. She wanted to respect family traditions and her grandmother, and also respect her own daughter's right to celebrate their special day how they wanted to. To her surprise, her grandmother shared her own frustration with the expectation of carrying on the 'family tradition' and was very supportive of this tradition becoming more flexible and not an expectation.

This may not be the case in every family, however, when we explore our feelings on a deeper level, we become clearer and more open to alternatives.

Sexuality

Sexuality can be a difficult topic to consider when you're thinking about your kids. Regardless of their age, parents generally don't want to think about their child having a sexuality. When a child comes out, it can feel like you are being forced to think about it. In most cases, sexuality is assumed to be straight, unless someone overtly fits the stereotypical mould of being gay. We also assume sexuality to be about sex. While this is true, sex is an element of sexuality, it is not all it is and it does not automatically mean your child is thinking about having sex.

We can often hold strong beliefs and values about sex and sexuality and when we assume them to be the same, it can make it more challenging to hear your child is not straight. The younger your child is when they come out, the harder that can be. One of the most common comments I hear from parents of kids under 18 is:

"They're too young to know. "

"They can't possibly know, as they haven't experienced it yet."

This directly results from inaccurate beliefs that we can't know what we like or are interested in without physical experience and that sexuality is about sex. Sexuality is about attraction before it's about sex. Many of us notice our attractions well before we understand what sex or sexuality is.

Don't panic. Like I said earlier, coming out does not mean your child is about to run off and have sex. However, it is important that you are open about this conversation so that they can talk with you without feeling shame or embarrassment, or support them to access the information they need to keep them safe, respectful, and respected. The alternative is they get their information from other sources that may not be accurate or tasteful. But that's a conversation for another day.

Like other conversations, please be mindful of your fears and concerns, so that you're not projecting those onto your child. For example, if you're worried about AIDS or other STIs, provide your child with the facts and strategies to protect themselves, rather than attempting to 'scare' them out of being sexually active.

Let's put this into perspective for a moment. Do you remember your very first crush? Who was it? How old were they? How old were you? Were you planning on having sex with them? Note, I said, planning, not dreaming. Your crush reflects your first attraction to another person. This is when you began to get a sense of your sexuality (consciously or unconsciously), whether it was the same as the societal messages you had received, or whether you felt different from what you believed to be expected of you. Not that everyone's first crush is a clear indicator of their sexuality, however, it can indicate to them they're feeling differently to what they witness in their lives or what is assumed of them. It's important to note that heterosexual people rarely think about this much, if at all, as there is nothing different. There is no need to examine how they're feeling. Alternatively, people experiencing same-sex attraction are more likely to notice they are feeling different, resulting in heightened awareness.

There are many deeply held beliefs and values around sex and sexuality and these can have a significant impact on how you feel, think and behave about your child's sexuality. You'll probably be aware of some, while others will fly under the radar. Now is the time to explore what they are, and where they've come from. Are they yours and do they still serve you?

Exploring your beliefs and values around gender and sexuality is a huge undertaking. We all have such a diverse range, which makes it impossible to cover them all in this book. My intent is for you to gain a deeper awareness and understanding so that you can make more informed decisions about your responses and whether you seek professional help to identify and work through them. Every parent I've worked with has been blindsided by at least a few of their own beliefs and values and the impact they were having on how they received the information about their child, as well as their day-to-day life. After we spent some time deepening their understanding, exploring what they were, their origins, effects and whether they aligned with how they wanted to be in the world, they could see more clearly and feel more able to be supportive of their child.

Below are some of the comments they shared at the end of this process that really stuck with me. These comments assured me that this is a necessary topic for this book and my programs offered to parents.

"I feel so much lighter. Life, in general, feels lighter, less over-whelming."

"I am shocked at how many subtle beliefs and values I've held. I'm so glad to be more aware and able to recognise why I feel the way I do about certain topics."

"I can't believe how much lighter I feel, especially given I didn't know I felt so heavy. I had no idea I had such deep ingrained beliefs."

"Wow!! Who knew that so many of the beliefs and values I had were not actually mine? I feel so much freer now that I can consciously create my own."

"I find it so much easier, now, to have some of those conversations that I used to feel were embarrassing or uncomfortable. I always knew it was important to have them with my child, so *they don't get all their information from the internet, but I didn't know how and it felt way too awkward. Sure, it's still a tad awkward, but it feels much more approachable."*

Beliefs and values can be overt, and they can be subtle in their presentation, they can be obvious, and they can catch us off guard. Often, we don't even realise that we have a particular belief or value, let alone how it influences our interactions with others. They can have a significant impact on all our relationships. I believe it's worth everyone doing a bit of a check-in, being curious and exploring what they believe, why they believe it and where it originated from. That's not to suggest you're wrong or need to change, however, once you've experienced this process, it is incredibly empowering to know that you are truly living by your own authentic beliefs and values about the world, the people in it and ensuring it all aligns with how you want to be.

MOP ~ Trust your heart and your body

This chapter may feel quite challenging and bring up a lot of emotions for you. If you scan your body, you might notice that you're holding some tension. Now is a good time to spend a few moments to connect with your body. Tensing and releasing can help you relax your muscles and feel more connected to your body. Often this exercise is offered as a progressive exercise of the whole body, from the feet all the way to the head. If you know it and would like to, go ahead, and do the whole body. Otherwise, for this mini mindfulness exercise, I'm going to show you how you can release some tension in just a few moments, at anytime, anywhere.

First, I invite you to scan your body. What do you notice? Are you holding any tension? No need to judge, criticise or adjust. Simply observe.

Begin by tensing your hands.

Spread your fingers wide, stretch your fingers as far as you can.

Hold for a couple of seconds.

Release

Repeat two more times.

Take in a deep breath, and as you exhale, let out a big sigh.

Move to your feet.

Tense your feet, try to spread your toes, stretch them as far as you can.

Hold for a couple of seconds.

Release

Repeat two more times.

Take in another deep breath, and as you exhale, let out a big sigh.

I invite you to scan your body again. What do you notice? Has anything changed?

If it feels helpful, write what you notice in your journal.

You can do this exercise anytime, anywhere. You can do any part of your body. Or your whole body, progressively. Whatever you feel you need and have the capacity for, in the moment.

Take Action ~ You've got this!

Who does it belong to?

Explore your own beliefs and values. Take some time to consider what they are, where they came from, whether they're yours and do they still serve you.

You know the drill by now. Make yourself a lovely nurturing beverage, find a comfy seat, and take some time out for yourself, preferably uninterrupted.

Take your journal/notepad and some pens or markers and begin to braindump all of your beliefs and values in relation to sexuality and gender. Try to write faster than your brain can think, so you can override the instinct to filter, judge or critique your thoughts.

Write until you've exhausted every possibility. When you think you're done...

Ask yourself – "And what else?"

Keep going until you've completely run out of things to write.

Go over your list and scan for any repeats. If there aren't any, I'd be concerned you still had your filter on, so ask yourself, one more time – "is there anything else?"

Create a table in your journal with the following (or similar) headings across the top.

Belief/Value

Origin

Is it mine?

Does it still serve me?

Record your beliefs and values in the first column.

That was the easy part. Next, I invite you to explore, one by one, where they came from. This can be a tough one because we are not usually conscious of where our beliefs and values come from. We just have them, and we live our life by them. Pop the answer in the 'Origin' column.

Some tips of where they may have come from are from your parents, grandparents, siblings, a teacher, coach, or religious leader. They may have come from something that you read or saw on TV or any number of other places. Do your best to explore the truth of where they came from, however, if you're uncertain, you can put down your best guess or leave it in the 'I don't know' pile.

Remember, while you're doing this, it is not about judging or criticising yourself or anyone else for these beliefs or values, it's simply getting to know them and their origins a little better.

The answers to the previous question may influence the next step. However, you can hold a belief or value that came from somewhere else and it still be yours. The trick is to get really honest with yourself and ask, is this truly mine, or do I have it because they passed it on to me? Again, no judgement. We all take on values and beliefs from others without considering them too much, if at all. Now is your opportunity to reflect and decide for yourself.

Complete your answers in the 'Is it mine?' column.

And finally, ask yourself 'Does it still serve me?' and include your response in the last column.

As I mentioned earlier, this can be a tough exercise and it may require some extra support. Don't be afraid to reach out for that support so you too can feel that freedom and lightness. So you can have open, honest conversations with your child and love and support them unconditionally. Untethered by uninvited or 'no longer suitable' beliefs and values.

Now, more than ever is a great time to allow yourself a moment of pause. You now have four under your belt, but I feel like the hard work you've just done deserves a bonus.

Bonus MOP

Bear Hug

Take a few minutes, or more if you have it, to simply breathe and give yourself a hug.

Stand tall, take a couple of deep breaths in, and allow the shoulders to release as you exhale.

Take your arms out to your sides, take in another deep breath, swing your arms in to grab hold of your shoulders, with your right arm on top, and exhale.

Take 5 deep breaths here.

You can close your eyes if that feels good.

Now repeat with your left arm on top.

Another gift you can give yourself, anytime you feel you need it.

Key Points

- Your beliefs and values impact how you support your child

- Be mindful of where your beliefs stem from

- Rekindle a connection with your child's true essence before the influences of societal limitations took hold.

- Opening your concept of family can allow you to release harmful beliefs that may distance you from your child.

- Sexuality is more than just sex. Narrowly defining it can hinder your ability to support and appreciate your child's identity.

Chapter 5

Thoughts

The Power Of Our Thoughts

"The way blue ocean water is reflection of sky, your actions are reflections of thoughts."

~ Amal Gade ~

Our beliefs and values influence our thoughts, but are they the only influence?

New research shows that humans have over six thousand thoughts per day. (Dr. Jordan Poppenk, 2020) That is an incredible number of thoughts, for one person, in one day. Does that surprise you? I know it surprised me when I first read it, but when I thought about it, it made sense. If we take a moment to contemplate, we get a snapshot of all the different things we have going on in life, the big and the small things. The truth is, unless we're exceptional meditators, our minds never stop. We're jumping from one thing to another or cycling through a few ruminating thoughts. "What's for dinner, where will we park, can I fit in a hair appointment next week, who will take on that new project at work, what will I give to my mother for her birthday?" and the list goes on and on.

Any wonder when we get new information about someone important to us, we feel overwhelmed. Now you have a bunch of new thoughts to add to the 6000 you already had going on. How can this be happening? Is it true? Is it a phase? How do they know? They're too young to know. Did I cause this? Who caused this? It's xxx fault. How will I support them? I have no idea about this stuff. I don't get it; they were xxx (insert a stereotype that goes against your child's identity, they've just shared) How will I tell xxx. What will xxx say? It's not safe for them to be out in the world in this way. What will happen to them? Will they be alone forever?

This is just to name a few of the hundreds, if not thousands, of new thoughts you have now added to your regime. These are perfectly normal and understandable. Some of these thoughts will be helpful and some will be unhelpful. Some will be necessary and some not. The timing of your thoughts will also vary in helpfulness.

In this chapter, we'll discuss some of the common thoughts parents have when their child first comes out, the impact our thoughts have on our emotions, and whether they are helpful.

How thoughts influence or impact emotions

There are different theories around whether our thoughts influence our emotions, or our emotions influence our thoughts. I believe, through years of observing human behaviour, including my own, that both have an element of truth. I believe that what you think, you will feel and I also believe that when you feel something, your cognitive mind makes sense of it through developing thoughts about it.

For the sake of this discussion, we're going to focus on how your thoughts impact your emotions, because our thoughts are powerful. We have the ability to change our mood and the way we feel, significantly, by altering our thoughts. Definitely easier said than done and not always possible. Give it a try. Check in with how you're currently feeling. Now think of something that you believe will conjure up the opposite feelings. For example, are you feeling reasonably happy? Now think about something that makes you unhappy. (be mindful not to go to the saddest or most unhappy thoughts and if you're currently depressed or your feeling quite down, skip this activity and just trust me. You can skip ahead to the second exercise) Spend a few minutes focusing on those thoughts. Repeating them over in your head. Delve right in. Now check in with yourself. How are you feeling? Has your mood changed?

Of course, I don't want to leave you feeling sad, so I encourage you to do the opposite now. Reassure yourself that you have just created those feelings and you don't need to continue to feel that way. You can focus your attention, now, on something that you love, that you're excited about or enjoy doing. Spend a few minutes on these thoughts until you feel lighter.

I'd like to note that unpleasant emotions are much more powerful than pleasant ones, which is related to our primal survival instinct. I'd also like to add that while our thoughts can be powerful, changing the way you feel will be much more effective when there is a change of behaviour, or action taken, along with the adaptation of thoughts. Therefore, you might find it helpful, in the above exercise, to stand up and move your body, do something that feels good in your body, alongside the uplifting thought injection. That might be dancing, going for a walk, or taking the action that is connected to your uplifted thought.

This exercise demonstrates how easily our thoughts can affect our emotions. Many of our 6,000 thoughts per day will not have any emotional attachment. They will be neutral. Like what we're having for dinner. Where will I put the pot plant I just bought? However, many of our thoughts do have an emotional impact and what we do with those thoughts can influence how we feel about ourselves, others, and our situation.

We can see another example of this in different people me may know. We all have those friends who seem to always be all 'doom and gloom', that see the downside in everything. You, or others, may have described them as 'glass half empty' type of people. On the other hand, there's those who do the opposite. They're always looking for the positive in a situation, more of a 'glass half full' type of person. You'll notice that the former often seem to be down, sad or in a low mood, whereas the latter are often upbeat and joyful, even in similar circumstances. I'm not suggesting this is easy and nor are we looking to criticise anyone. This is more of an observation of the impact of attitude and self-talk.

*** Please note; we're not referring to people who are experiencing depression or other mental illness here.

The important thing is that you understand that your thoughts, mind and behaviour, can influence how you feel. This suggests the importance of taking action to process your behaviour, thoughts and feelings openly and freely with some-one who is outside your family and you can feel safe and comfortable with. I also like to assure people that I work with that thoughts are not negative or positive. They all have their place and purpose. It's more about whether they're helpful. And it's often not that the specific thought is unhelpful, rather what we do with it. Let's delve into some examples and find some ways to ease your mind a little.

Be present with what your child is telling you now. Avoid jumping ahead.

The adult brain, as we've discussed, is incredibly busy (6,000 plus thoughts a day) and, some might say, overactive. This is where the breathing exercises we've been practicing will come in handy. They're not just because I enjoy meditation and yoga, though that is true, it's because I know it's effective for everyone in reducing stress, anxiety and overwhelm.

It's easy to get carried away with the 'what if's' and the possi-bilities for your child's future. Whether that's thinking about their safety, happiness, relationships, or medical care, or how this might affect you and/or other family members. All these are valid concerns and considerations and will require some time, energy, and attention at some stage. However, when experiences feel overwhelming, the most helpful thing you can do is stay present, stay with the current facts and situation, and avoid jumping ahead and falling into the worry about the future. I know, I know, easier said than done. Your child needs you to stay present with what they're telling you, rather than rushing ahead to worrying about the possibilities in the future.

Now is a good time to practice one of those MOPs we've learned so far. You can start by connecting to your breath and allowing a longer exhale to your inhale. Or take a look back to remind you of one of your favourites.

Now ask yourself, what is important at this moment? What does my child need right now? What do I need right now? And do that. Your child has just told you some news that was potentially tough to hear (or perhaps you've known for a while. Wherever you're at on this journey you and your child will benefit from this). It was also tough for them to say. They need you to be there with them, in this moment, hold space for them, stay present and contain the mind spiralling. Again, I know this is easier said than done and I'm not asking you to ignore your feelings. Ask yourself, "What's happening now?" That's what matters. You might need to take a moment for yourself. You might need to access some support to work through this. That is perfectly okay. In fact, I wish more people would give themselves that gift, so they can work through the process much faster, smoother and with less hurt and pain.

Struggling to understand

"I don't understand", or a version of this statement is something I hear all the time. Parents are sometimes referring to not understanding about sexuality or gender identity, or how this is possible for their child, and other times their struggle is not understanding their own feelings and response to the news. Either way, it can leave you with feelings of inadequacy as a parent, or an inability to be fully supportive. Parents often share that it can lead them to question everything about being a parent, their understanding of the world, of their child.

You might not understand, yet. And this can feel quite foreign. You may never completely understand, but you will improve your understanding significantly in time. It's hard to undo the many years of explicit and implicit learning, but it is possible. Remember, you don't have to understand to be loving and supportive. Take a deep breath and give yourself the space to learn.

Over the last ten to fifteen years, the landscape of language and identity has shifted significantly. That can make it feel like a more difficult space for parents to navigate, worrying about what language they should use. This is evident, particularly in young people, as they are very articulate about their identities and are also better at connecting with and communicating their thoughts and feelings about them. We could link this to access to internet and social media, both of which are spaces where they can significantly explore identity before sharing with their parents.

These shifts, along with their child's clarity in their identity and the way their feeling, can leave parents feeling ill informed, confused, and uncertain about how to communicate with their child. This is one of the key elements of why I wrote this book and created programs for parents. So I can support them to catch up, to gain some clarity and confidence, and to feel more able to unconditionally love and support their child. This won't happen overnight, however following the steps, with guidance and support, parents gain more clarity and confidence as they increase their understanding of the facts and nuances of sexuality and gender identity. Once they have that understanding, they can then begin to explore and deepen their understanding of theirs and their child's experiences and emotions. My aim is always to support and encourage families to build their relationships, deepen their connections, and create environments for healthy, vibrant, loving individuals to thrive.

Role Reversal

An element of the struggle for parents, in this context, is the uninvited, unintended, often unwelcome, feeling of a role reversal. Until a certain point in their child's life, it's a parent's role to be the 'knowing' one, older, wiser, and more experienced in life. For all parents, at some stage that changes, however, it's not usually until later. There is a stage during adolescence where teenagers may think this has changed, however, that's more about them no longer being prepared to take their parents' advice, unquestioned or unchallenged. While this is also a difficult stage for parents to navigate, it's an important stage for their development of independence, but that's for another book. When this shift in roles comes totally unexpected, like when a child comes out, it can come as a bit of a shock, and be difficult for parents to navigate.

You may have experienced this on some level, where your child has shared information with you about their sexuality or gender identity and you feel totally helpless. Instead of you being the one with all the information and life experience for them to turn to, they're now the expert. The one with the information and the experience (unless you are LGBTQ+ yourself). You don't have all the answers and, in fact, some of the information you have might be inaccurate or out of date. They may not be asking you for guidance. They may have sourced that from elsewhere before they told you. That can be hard to swallow.

I want to assure you that while you may feel totally out of your element; it doesn't need to stay that way. Over time, with support and access to up to date, accurate information, you can catch up. It can also be quite humbling and character building to get comfortable not being in the driver's seat. Do your research and learn more about your child's identity and other elements of being LGBTQ+ so that you can go on the journey with them. Don't let your fear of not knowing impede you from finding out more.

What is even more powerful is to catch up to your child's level of self-awareness and personal insight. One of the incredible elements of my job, working with young LGBTQ+ people, was witnessing this in them. For most LGBTQ+ folk, they've had to do a lot of soul searching, digging deep inside, asking themselves a lot of questions, getting to know themselves on a much deeper level than many, as they came to terms with their sexuality/gender identity. Much of this has occurred prior to them sharing with anyone else.

LGBTQ+ people are required to explore themselves on a much deeper level than most cisgender and straight people, at a much earlier age, to prepare for the outside world and the questions, judgements, and challenges it will throw at them (or present them with). They want to be clear about what they're feeling so they don't put themselves through the pain and struggles of coming out unnecessarily. It's part of their preparation and protection for what might occur.

This sort of exploration of identity is something we can all benefit from. Deepening your understanding of yourself, and developing your personal insight, is one of the most empowering experiences you can gift yourself. You'll not only have a deeper connection with yourself, but you'll also deepen your understanding and connection with loved ones.

Witnessing families come together in this way is one of the most rewarding, heart-warming experiences of my career. I feel so much gratitude to those individuals and families for allowing me to walk this journey with them and trusting me to guide them through the process. It is truly beautiful.

What also happens as you do this work is you let go of some of those expectations of yourself as a parent. You realise you can be a loving, caring, effective and supportive parent without being the expert. Without having all the answers. In fact, you can do a much better job if you're able to invite your child to be an equal participant in that relationship. Trusting their ability to know what they're feeling and creating space for them to explore. Allowing them and yourself to feel safe, to try new things, to be wrong and to gently challenge what doesn't feel right. This can bring a truly magical parenting experience.

I want to acknowledge that this is not how most of us were brought up, or how we learned to parent, so it will probably feel foreign and uncomfortable, hence the encouragement to do it with support.

I'd also like to note that although your child may know much more about sexuality and/or gender identity than you, depending on their age, they may not be fully equipped to recognise or identify risks, particularly predatory behaviours (this is for all children, regardless of sexuality or gender identity). The more you can grow and develop your knowledge and understanding of your child's experience, the more able you will be to differentiate between real and perceived danger. If you trust your child's expertise around their sexuality and gender identity, they will be more able to come to you and listen to you.

Perception of self as a parent

Have you ever cringed as you've spoken and realised you sounded exactly like your parents? One of the principal places we learn our parenting style is from our own parents or carers. We think that we've made a conscious decision to do the same, the opposite, or a combination of both, as our parents. However, the dynamics of the relationship between us and our child, combined with the dynamics of the other parent, if they're involved, can often challenge our ideal for how we thought we would act as a parent.

Parenting is truly the most important job any of us will ever do and whilst there are 100s of books on how to be a good parent, there are none that train us to be parents to our own children. It is also one of the most judged and criticised jobs on earth. Everybody has an opinion and thinks they know best. People are not shy in sharing those opinions, and strangely, often without all the information. There's a lot of pressure to 'get it right', however, you'll never please everyone. What's right to one person will be wrong to another.

I remember my experience parenting as a young mum. Everyone had an opinion, and they weren't shy to share it, often in a not very encouraging way. I felt a load of judgement, which caused me to be reluctant to ask for help. I always felt like it was because I was young, and whilst that had an impact, I've since learned that my experience is common among parents of any age. Age was just the excuse people used to tell me what I was doing wrong, to judge and criticise me. I remember wishing these people could share their knowledge and experience in a more supportive and encouraging way. Creating a safe space for open conversation and exploration of different ideas. I would've felt less alone and isolated. Don't get me wrong, there were a couple of key support people there for me, though the harsher voices were much louder.

I'm sure the urge to judge is born from our expectations of what it is to be a good parent. The fears that are carried within most of us, as parents. The fear of messing things up or harming our kids. Your child's sexuality or gender identity is no different. It's simply another platform for people to judge, criticise, and share their uninvited opinions on parenting. I've heard some awful stories from parents I've worked with over the years. The horrid things that people say, with little to no accurate information. I won't repeat those things here, as those people don't deserve the airspace, however, I have no doubt you know exactly what I'm talking about.

These external voices can have an enormous impact on how well you think you are going as a parent. Setting some boundaries and making choices about how and with whom you spend your time can help minimise the impact they will have. However, what I feel is even more valuable to reflect on is your own voice. How are you talking to and about yourself as a parent? Those external voices can be loud, upsetting, frustrating, and hard to ignore. However, what is even louder and harder to ignore is your own voice. There is no escape. It is with you 24/7. So, if you can't get some kindness and compassion flowing towards yourself, you're going to have a rather dim perception of yourself as a parent.

Let's get something straight (no pun intended). Kindness and compassion towards yourself is different from excusing poor behaviour. It's not a free ticket to continue to mess up, and it's not a request for your child to forgive you. Forgiveness is a process, so you need to give your child space to be angry, upset, or frustrated at your former self. Approaching yourself with kindness and compassion is an acknowledgment that you are and have done the best that you could with what you had at any point in time. And you will continue to learn, grow, and practice what's required of you to be the best parent you can be. And that's exactly why you're here, reading this book.

Bonus action: give yourself a hug and acknowledge that you're on a journey of learning how to best support your child. You might also like to take Elizabeth Gilbert's advice, below."Wh atever you do, try not to dwell too long on your failures. You don't need to conduct autopsies on your disasters." ~ Elizabeth Gilbert

Your perception of yourself as a parent will affect how you feel tremendously. (See the end of this chapter for an activity on how to improve your perception) As you might realise by now, your thoughts will directly impact how you feel. If you tell yourself over and over that you're an idiot, you're a terrible parent and you've got no idea what you're doing, you're going to feel pretty ordinary. On the flip side, if you repeatedly tell yourself that you've and are growing, you'll notice a little smile appear on your face and start to feel more uplifted. If this is completely new to you, it might take a little while for you to believe it, but with persistence and support, it can happen.

I'm not suggesting you ignore the truth or the reality of your behaviour. Being able to acknowledge you made mistakes, without justifying or excusing them, means you have the capacity to grow as a parent and a human being. Alternatively, refusing to see your flaws is unhelpful. The difference here is recognising and responding accordingly to your behaviours, not labelling yourself, because of those behaviours. For example, "That was a poor parenting decision", as opposed to "I am a terrible parent". Brené Brown, a professor, social worker, author, and researcher, known for her research on shame, vulnerability, and leadership, talks about this being the difference between experiencing guilt and shame. A focus on behaviour, results in feelings of guilt and a focus on self, results in feelings of shame. Guilt is helpful for behaviour change and shame is not.

Your perception of yourself will not only affect how you feel about yourself, it'll also affect your child, other family members, and everyone you meet. Consider, for a minute. If you're feeling good about yourself as a parent, how do you think that influences your behaviour? Particularly towards your child. If you feel confident, clear, and assured in your decision making, behaviour, interactions with, and your capacity to empathise and hear your child, that is definitely going to improve your relationship and connection with them. Alternatively, if you're second guessing yourself, doubting or judging yourself, that will also filter through to your relationship with them and create distance between the two of you.

Please note, in the above paragraph, I am talking to those who are working towards being loving and supportive parents of their LGBTQ+ child. Not those who are trying to change their child and/or completely opposed to their identity.

If you are still processing your child's news about their sexuality and/or gender identity, this is different. You need to allow yourself the space to work through it (and ensure you are actively working through it). Part of this process is to accept where you are in the process and know that you are working toward accepting and celebrating your child and yourself.

Your dreams for your child.

Over the years of working with hundreds of young LGBTQ+ people, the vast majority were happy with who they were. There was no problem with their sexuality or gender identity, their struggles were more about how others would or did respond and treat them. From my experience, when they felt unconditionally loved and supported exactly how they were, they thrived. Behaviours at home and in school, their mood and confidence all improved out of sight. A variety of research also confirms this. LGBTQ+ people succeed in all areas of life and one of the noticeable contributing factors is a loving, supportive network of people around them.

You likely had hopes and dreams for your child, and they may not align with this new information you have about them. Regardless of your child's sexuality or gender identity, this still may have been the case. This may be a shock to you. It's important to realise that your hopes and dreams for your child will affect how you imagined their life would be and how you perceive their gender and sexuality, will also affect how you respond.

Prior to them coming out, these perceptions of their sexuality, gender identity, and future may have been on a subconscious level, and it is now brought to the conscious. It's natural for your mind to go into overdrive, trying to make sense of it all. It's natural for you to be scanning past experiences, behaviours, and other indicators, attempting to gather evidence that either contradicts or reinforces what they've told you. You might also question why you didn't know.

I wonder if you can relate to any of these statements or questions I've heard from other parents?

"But she's always been so feminine. How can she be a boy?"

"But he's always been into boys' things. How can he be a girl?"

"He has so many female friends. They all love him. He can't be gay."

"She's had boyfriends since she started high school. Why would she suddenly say she's gay?"

"How will she ever be able to get married if she likes both genders? She'll be alone forever."

"She/he has never given any indication that this is how they feel. I would've known."

"I knew she loved to play boys' sports and was never comfortable in dresses, but I just thought she was a tomboy."

"He's always been more effeminate than his brother, but I thought he was going to be gay, not trans."

"Why does he have to be bi? It means he likes girls, right? Then he can just have relationships with girls."

Does any of this sound familiar? It's exhausting, right?! That's the consistent message I've received from parents. They're constantly analysing, assessing, trying to figure out what they missed, whether this is real, and how can it be true. Any wonder they feel confused, overwhelmed, and exhausted. It also prevents them from being present with their child and able to hear and understand their experience. All these questions, plus others, spinning around in their minds, create a block to being able to truly hear and begin the process of understanding their child and their own feelings.

All these questions and statements are buying into the stereotypes of gender and sexuality. Stereotypes of the ideal life have a lot of influence over our hopes and dreams and thoughts. I remember, just before Covid, one parent of a trans girl (assigned male at birth) struggled to believe that their child was trans because they still loved football and wanted a new membership that year. Right at the beginning of one of her sessions with me, she stated, "I was right, she's not trans. She asked for a football membership for her birthday." The look on this mother's face, after the words came out of her mouth, was heartbreaking. She then broke down, crying.

This family had been on a journey for about 12 months. The parents struggled to understand in the beginning, however, had done a lot of work and were feeling reasonably comfortable in their understanding. There had been many steps taken, and this mother felt like she was 100% supportive. They had been doing great. Their child was happy and thriving. They were happy the overwhelm had significantly reduced after about 2 months of working through one of my programs. She had started advocating for her child and was planning to attend her first LGBTQ+ event.

What she realised at that moment, during our session, was that she was still holding onto hope that things would change. Her unconscious assumptions about gender, the deep beliefs that were in alignment with gender stereotypes, were silently sabotaging the work she'd been doing. She was unconsciously scanning for evidence to prove her child was not trans. This was a breakthrough moment for her. As a feminist and an avid football fan herself, she realised how strange it was to assume that her child must be male because she still liked football. "This is not only outdated and ridiculous, it's totally contradictory to my own personal beliefs and experiences", she stated.

Later in that session, she shared with me that she realised, as soon as she heard her own words, that this was not reasonable. However, it also enabled her to recognise the power of her thoughts. As soon as her daughter requested the membership, she began a loop thought pattern of, "She's not trans, she still likes football". She had convinced herself that this was true, despite her cognitive understanding to the contrary. Once she said it out loud, she could interrupt that loop with some "common sense" (her words) and continue to work through her feelings about her daughter.

A couple of months later she shared, with a bit of a giggle, "You know that ludicrous day, where I 'kinda' lost my mind a little, it was the best day ever. Even though I thought I was okay, I realised I was still hanging on to hope that she would change her mind and I know that while ever I did that, I wouldn't be able to be there for her one hundred percent. I feel so much lighter now."

I disagree with her, that she had lost her mind. I would say she had become more in tune with it. I understand, though, why she felt that way and she is definitely not alone. That is a common statement I hear from parents. "I feel like I'm losing my mind." It is simply an overwhelming time that is difficult to put the pieces together, alone.

Is it a phase?

But isn't it just a phase?

This is one of the most common questions I get asked about LGBTQ+ young people. "Isn't it just a phase?" "Couldn't it be a stage they are going through?" "Didn't we all go through stages of experimentation?" "I remember when I was younger, I kissed a girl at a party, and it was kind of exciting. Isn't this just like that?" "They're a teenager/child/young adult. Isn't it normal to experiment?"

Or it can be that the person is older, and the questions are more like, "Is this a midlife crisis?" or "Are they just reacting to..." {insert stressful or traumatic experience} or "Are they just trying to get back at me?" {or someone else in their life, perhaps an ex-partner}

We all go through a variety of phases in our lives, and this may or may not be a phase for your child. Due to the challenging nature of coming out, for most people, it is unlikely to be. I understand the attraction to this thought. It would mean life can go back to the way things were before. It may be the only thing that makes sense to you right now. Regardless, it is important to understand that it is how your child is feeling currently and they need you to trust that they know how they feel and continue to love and support them.

If it is a phase, it will pass much more smoothly if they have your support, while they explore their identity and how they are feeling. There is no harm in allowing them the space to figure this out.

Now, let's consider the alternative. It's not a phase. The chances are they have been thinking about this for a very long time, and have been rehearsing this conversation with you repeatedly. It took an enormous amount of courage to tell you. Regardless of their age, you are one of the most important people in their lives and they want your love, support, approval, and acceptance. The risks are very real for them. They have a lot to lose if you're not okay and they can never know until they tell you.

Let's consider how your child may feel. They tell you something important about themselves and you don't believe them. I know this can be difficult. You want the best for your child. You want to protect them and keep them safe. You want to help them make 'sensible', responsible choices in their lives. And as we've recently discussed, most parents have hopes and dreams for their children and perhaps this news doesn't quite fit.

Now imagine how they might feel if they tell you this important information and you DO believe them, or at least you don't question them or tell them "It's just a phase". It may be too late for that. You may be reading this after your child came out, and you told them you thought it was just a phase. That's okay. An apology for the doubt, criticism, or disagreeing with them can go a long way, while you work your way towards a deeper understanding.

My tips –

1. If you feel like it might be a phase, keep it to yourself. If you need to talk it through with someone, see tip three.

2. Keep in mind "What if it isn't a phase?" What is most important; Your child's health and well-being, or being right?

3. Talk to someone!!! Be mindful not to share your child's personal information without their permission. If they've told no one else, you might have to seek professional support to ensure their privacy. (You can email me for your free Guide to finding a support person)

4. Avoid colluding with other family members or friends. We can always find evidence to prove things we want to prove. We can't argue with how another person feels, even if others agree with us.

5. Remember, phases have a time limit, so if you're convinced it is a phase, it will pass. In the meantime, refer to the above tips.

The bottom line is, it may or may not be a phase, though it is unlikely, due to the challenging nature of coming out. If it is a phase, it will pass, and your support will mean a lot to your child. If it's not, the hurt caused by continuing to overtly not believe them may not pass. Your child's mental and emotional health is more important than you being right. Get the support you need and avoid falling into the trap of colluding with other family members and friends.

They're too young to know

Perhaps you didn't even get to the 'phase' question. You might feel that they're too young to know. I have spoken with parents of 5-year-olds, through to 18-year-olds who have felt their child was too young or too inexperienced to know. If you're not comfortable or want things to be different, it's natural for you to look for a reason this can't be true, and age and life experience might be the most obvious. We say it about many things in relation to children, teenagers, and young adults. Except, often we're wrong. Or at least, not quite right. I try to remind myself, just because they're young, doesn't mean they don't know things. It doesn't mean they don't know how they feel. It means they need space and support to figure things out.

Do you remember a time when you were young, and you shared something about yourself with an adult and they told you that you were too young to know, that you were wrong? How did that feel? I know some of these circumstances may have turned out to be true, however many wouldn't, and the way it made you feel certainly wasn't good. Adults often assume that if a child can't articulate their feelings, then they mustn't be real. The truth is, kids often have a good idea about how they feel, though struggle to put it into words. Developmentally, children are likely (depending on age) still developing their ability to connect language to their feelings. Allowing them the freedom of expression is more important than labels and words.

Children know from as young as two, what their gender is. Some will articulate it clearly and some won't, for a variety of reasons. Some won't realise until they're much older. Neither is more valid than the other. They are just different. The same goes for sexuality. Some children realise their sexuality is different to heterosexual before they know what sexuality is. Sexuality is not all about sex, it is about their feelings, their attractions.

If you're stuck thinking your child is too young to know, or it's just a phase, it makes it difficult for you to be open to hearing about your child's feelings and experiences and supporting them to safely explore their identity. A lack of effective communication will only exacerbate your concern and overwhelm you. No one wants to think about their 11-year-old and sex in the same thought. And it's hard to consider your 8-year-old travelling the tough road of a trans child. All parents want the best for their kids and that includes taking the path that seems to be the safest, easiest, highest possibility for success. We often hear that being LGBTQ+ isn't the easiest path. However, it's a lot worse for LGBTQ+ kids who have to hide who they are, and the road is certainly a lot easier and safer when parents and families are supportive and loving.

Lauren and Jake

About 5 years ago, Lauren reached out to me, as her 11-year-old son Jake had just informed her he was being bullied at school for being gay. He was confused about why the other kids would be so mean, "just because of who I am". (I'm with Jake). Aside from being devastated that her son was being bullied, she was also confused as to how he could know he's gay at such a young age. She was also worried he was just copying good family friends of theirs, whom he idolises. (we'll talk more about that in the next section)

Lauren expressed her struggles to me in our first conversation. "How can he possibly know he's gay at his age? He's had no experience, and he's too young to even know about sex. We have a fairly open family, and we talk about all kinds of things, but he doesn't 'really' understand what sex is, yet. I'm convinced he's just copying Carl and Geoff because he loves them, and they love him so much. I'm worrying that perhaps we shouldn't have let him spend so much time with them. But that would be sad because they love each other and have so much fun together." You can see Lauren's dilemma.

Lauren's son Jake first mentioned being gay, when he was 8, but she brushed it off, thinking he's just heard the word and copying their friends who'd been over for a dinner party the night before. As with most 8-year-olds, it was a brief conversation. Lauren smiled, and before she could say anything, he went on to the next activity. Jake never mentioned it again, and she thought little more about it, continuing to allow him to play dress-ups and express himself however he felt comfortable.

You can imagine her surprise when Jake came home upset about being bullied "because of the way he is." Lauren enquired with Jake what he meant by "because of the way he is" and his response was, "for being gay. Remember I told you when I was 8 that I'm like Geoff and Carl?"

When Lauren tried to explain to Jake that being gay is "an adult thing", he became quite upset and yelled at her and cried. She was shocked, confused, and very concerned about Jake. She comforted him and told him she'd contact the school to ensure they put a stop to the bullying. This seemed to appease Jake, for the time being, though Lauren knew this was not the end of it and she had to do something quick.

No one's to blame

When Lauren called my office, she was feeling quite distressed. Bouncing between disbelief and self-blame. As I mentioned earlier, she was concerned Jake had confused his connection with their gay friends with being gay himself. This is a common misconception parents experience, looking for blame or explanation. Something they did, or someone else did, to cause their child to be trans or gay.

I want to assure you that you can't make someone gay or trans. Simply put, it is the way they are, the way they feel. No one can cause someone to feel that way. The likely truth for Jake is that he connected so deeply with Carl and Geoff because he could see a part of himself in them. This is a blessing for Jake, as many kids go through their entire childhood never seeing or meeting anyone like them, which can be detrimental to their well-being and social development.

Parents find all sorts of ways to blame themselves or others. Examples of comments I've heard from parents are:

"*I knew I shouldn't have let him do dance classes. I should've insisted he play football or baseball.*"

"*I should've insisted she wear dresses sometimes and put more effort into teaching her how to use makeup and all the girly things. I was just never very good at it.*"

"*I should've made sure he had more male influence in his life.*"

"*I should've been more strict and not let her spend so much time playing with the neighbourhood boys. It wouldn't have hurt her* to *have more girlfriends, she just never seemed to gravitate to girls."*

"When her mother died, I was not very present. I didn't realise how much she was missing out on. I should've had more women visiting and teaching her all that girly stuff, and then she might not crave female attention now."

And remember Josie and Paul – she blamed herself for being a single mother and Paul growing up in a house full of females and not enough male influence.

"I can't help but think I should've stayed with his dad, so he could've had more male influence, even though it wasn't a healthy or safe (for me) household."

None of these things caused their kids to be gay or trans. There is nothing wrong with them, so there is no one to blame and no need to find an 'explanation' for it.

It didn't take much to reassure Lauren that she hadn't caused her son to be gay by allowing him to experience the loving, caring, and fun relationship he had with their good friends. In her heart, she knew this to be true. She was a front row witness to the joy that their connection brought them all. The guys were also able to support her to realise this by sharing some of their own childhood experiences and their wish that they had healthy role models in their lives as they were growing up.

There was a bit more work to do for Lauren to understand how Jake could be so sure about his sexuality, without having had any intimate experiences and being so young. The intellectual learning came fairly quickly, however, the 'felt' learning took longer.

It's common for parents to have the cognitive understanding, but still struggle to feel comfortable with what their mind tells them to be true. Lauren understood children can have a crush or a physical feeling about another person, without acting on it, before they understand exactly what same-sex attraction is and without having had any physical experiences, however, the concept of her son knowing his sexuality was still hard.

Together, we created a safe space for her to explore all her feelings about the possibility her son was gay. What she was thinking (telling herself) and what her concerns were. She needed to feel safe to work through her thoughts and feelings and not have them judged or criticised by her or anyone else.

And then began the rollercoaster of emotions fed by all the thoughts about what might happen to him, what his life might be like and whether he'll be happy. We'll talk more about that in the next chapter.

I've noticed, over the years that with sexuality and gender identity, adults get too caught up in the 'grown-up brain', worrying about the future, all the possibilities, what happens next, and not enough attention to exactly what their child is telling them. What their experience means for them at this moment in time. Adult brains overcomplicate things, causing them a lot more stress than might be necessary at that moment.

Of course, this is perfectly normal. There are a lot of things to consider, particularly if your child has come out as trans, however practising the MOPs that I've shared in this book will help you stay more present and ease any unnecessary stress. There is no point in worrying about hormones if your child is only six and there's no need to worry about becoming a grandparent if they're 12. Do your best to be present with what your child is telling you now, what they need at this moment, and how you can best support them.

I want to take a moment to acknowledge that I've only touched on a handful of the bazillion thoughts that could run through your head. I hope you find them helpful along with the process we go through. If I didn't address your concerning thoughts, please reach out so we can work through them together. It'll also be helpful for me to know for future books. It's important to me you feel heard and represented and if you're feeling it, others will be too.

MOP ~ Trust your heart and your body

Shoulder Shrug

Shrug your shoulders up to your ears.

Hold for the count of three.

Allow them to drop.

Repeat.

This time inhale with a shrug.

Hold your breath as you hold the shrug (count to 3)

Exhale with a sigh as you release your shoulders.

Relax your jaw, and allow it to lower so you can feel a gap between the back of your teeth.

Release your eyebrows.

Repeat the shoulder shrug, including the breath, relaxed jaw and eyebrow release (1 - 3 times)

Notice what you feel...

If it feels helpful, write it in your journal.

Take Action ~ You've got this!

Adjusting your perception of yourself as a parent.

Regardless of whether you're completely awful to yourself or if you feel you're usually kind, except in relation to your child's sexuality or gender identity, it won't hurt to take some steps to improve.

Take out your notebook and let's reflect.

What is your perception? What kinds of words do you use to talk to and about yourself in relation to being a parent? (Write these down) Ensure you include the off-the-cuff statements you'd consider not serious. They all count.

On a scale of 0 – 10, how would you rate your level of kindness to yourself?

How would your best friend rate you as a parent?

How much difference is there between your rating and your friends? What can you do to work towards bringing those closer together? (and no, I don't mean alter your friend's rating)

What's the most common unhelpful word/s you use? What different, kinder word/s could you use?

Practice more of those.

Please note, you can do this exercise on your own. However, as with most of these types of exercises, it is more effective for digging deeper when you have a witness, and even better with a knowledgeable professional.

Key Points

- Your thoughts impact/influence your emotions.

- Be present with your child – avoid jumping ahead.

- It's okay to struggle to understand. You can be loving and supportive without understanding.

- Role reversal feels uncomfortable, however, it's a normal part of parenting.

- Your perception of self as a parent will affect your behaviour. Be kind to yourself.

- Your dreams for your child are not their dreams. You may need to let them go.

- It's unlikely to be a phase, however, it's important to trust they know how they feel, at this moment and support them.

- They're never too young to know how they feel, including if they're too young to understand or articulate it.

- There's nothing wrong with them, so no one's to blame.

Chapter 6

Emotions

Feeling all the feels

"May your choices reflect your hopes, not your fears."

~ Nelson Mandala ~

Riding the rollercoaster

What I'm about to tell you might be a surprise, however, I'm going to tell you anyway, because I believe it to be true and crucial to our healing.

There's no such thing as a negative, bad, or wrong emotion.

All emotions are valid and necessary. It's what we do with them that counts. Emotions are different to behaviours. For example, anger is an emotion and can be useful. Aggression is a behaviour. One is ok, the other is not.

Now, I didn't say they're all pleasant, that you want them, or you must enjoy them all, but they all have their place. Of course, some emotions feel better than others and are therefore more welcome. With the unpleasant ones, we tend to drown in them, react to them or push them away, ignore them or pretend they're not there. The problem with this approach is it doesn't work. Not in the long term, at least. They will always come back and bite you, often at the most inappropriate time. Mostly because anytime feels like an 'inappropriate' time to feel the tough emotions. Feeling, rather than rejecting these unpleasant emotions is crucial, as you often can't reach acceptance and comfort without going through this process.

"What are we meant to do with them?" I hear you ask. The short answer is, give them the space they need. Allow them to be there. Let go of the fight. This allows you a much greater chance of working through them so that you can heal, process, and release them. I know, I know, like much of what I talk about in this book, 'much easier said than done'. But it is possible. I'll share some strategies in this chapter and, of course, I'd be happy to support you to work through them in one of my programs if you'd like to fast-track the process.

What are the emotions that are swirling around in your body? Let's talk about the ones that come up consistently for almost every parent I work with. That's right, you're not alone in how you're feeling. There are, of course, other emotions that come up for people, as everyone's experience is unique. You may experience some or all of these.

- Grief, for the dreams you had for your child and/or feeling like your child, as you knew them, is gone.

- Guilt and/or embarrassment about how you're feeling and/or your behaviour or responses to your child coming out

- Sadness

- Fear and worry about your child, yourself, your family, how to talk to your child, and how to communicate with others.

Grief

Are you feeling that your:

- Dreams for your child are lost?

- Your child, as you knew them, is gone?

Grief is not one emotion on its own. We can feel a bunch of different emotions inside of grief and all of them are okay. They're normal. You might experience sadness, fear, anger, guilt, confusion, frustration, or even relief or gratitude, once you've processed. We experience grief for all sorts of losses and while one of the most painful losses is the death of a loved one; it is not the only way we experience grief. Grief is an ordinary human response to any loss.

I'd like to clear one thing up here before we go any further. You CAN experience grief after your child comes out. In fact, it is common. I know it is quite controversial in some circles, including some parent support groups. I also realise some parents struggle to name what they're feeling as grief because their child is still alive, and they don't want to be disrespectful to those who have lost a child. What I'd like you to understand is:

- Grief is a response to loss, any perceived loss.

- Grief is a process... a healthy process that we have to go through.

- One person's grief does not take away from another person's grief.

- Even if you consider your loss to be less than someone else's, this doesn't invalidate your experience or mean you're not experiencing grief.

- Your grief is valid.

- Grief is a helpful process. When embraced, it is a road to healing and acceptance.

After a child (of any age) comes out, it's common for parents to go through a grieving process and the emotions attached are similar to any other grieving process. You may be feeling like the dreams and hopes you had for your child are lost or you might feel like the child you had is gone, particularly if they're transgender. These feelings deserve the time, attention, space and compassion that they need. Like any grieving process, it is important to allow that process to take its course with support and loving kindness to yourself.

It's probably a good idea to intermittently engage the support of a more objective person to ensure you neither push yourself through the process too fast and/or get stuck. The grief process can be more potent and therefore more effective and healing when we have a witness.

It is true, your child is still here, therefore you should be mindful of how you speak about your grief to them. It can feel challenging for your child to hear about your grief. That, of course, doesn't negate your feelings, it simply highlights that it is not their responsibility to help you work through your feelings.

Take some time to reflect on what the grief is about. Sometimes, when I'm working with parents, they arrive thinking that they're grieving one thing and realise after some time talking it through and checking in with themselves that it is actually something else entirely. Often parents realise they don't need to lose (or aren't actually losing) the thing they were worried about losing. Or the initial grief helps us uncover grief or loss that's been hidden. It's often the case, as we dig deeper, we end up feeling freer, more content than we have in years.

It may have changed shape a little, but it can still be there. Other times, parents realise they had a bunch of unconscious expectations for their child's future that were not in alignment with their child's hopes, regardless of their sexuality and gender identity, therefore they would not come to fruition, anyway. Remember our discussion about hopes and dreams... there is grief connected to these too.

For parents of gender-diverse kids, grieving the son or daughter you feel you've lost can be tough. And like other grief, it's not necessarily a 'one off', linear experience. Grief and its processing can come intermittently. Sometimes we work through it, and feel better, only to notice something else pops up. It's like our psyche needs a little hiatus to do some unconscious processing prior to taking the next step. Pushing it aside for a while is also okay, as we sometimes need to wait until we're ready and have the space. Different things will also likely come up at different times and stages of your child's life, which makes it even more important to process your grief earlier, rather than trying to ignore or dismiss it. This will help you manage what comes up in the future, more effectively and with less struggle.

Parents of trans kids that I work with often talk about the struggle between feeling like they've lost a son or daughter, and also gained one. The confusion, internal conflict and emotional rollercoaster can feel too much, sometimes. Understanding that it is the meaning you put on having a daughter or son that creates many of these feelings, can help create a shift. I work through this with parents, encouraging them to reflect on what it means to them to have a son/daughter. What they're most worried about losing or changing, and then acknowledging the enormity of this experience. This process takes time, however, it's a tremendous step towards healing.

Sadness

I'm often asked, "Is it wrong to feel sad about my child's sexuality or gender identity?"

The short answer is no! It's absolutely not wrong to feel sad. In fact, it is perfectly normal and very common.

Sadness can show up in a variety of forms and for different reasons. Like other emotions, it's closely connected to your thoughts and beliefs. Your thoughts and what you believe can influence how you feel. That's not to suggest it is easy to turn your sadness on or off, however, you may have more influence over how you feel than you think.

I encourage you to explore where your sadness is coming from. What is it truly about? As we've discussed, often we think we know where our feelings come from, only to realise later, it is different or more complex than what we thought. When we have a clear understanding, it makes it more possible to offer ourselves the compassion we need and the space to work through those feelings.

Is your sadness about you feeling like you'll miss a particular part of your child or an experience you thought you would have with them? Is it you feel sad about the struggles you anticipate they'll experience? Or they won't wear your favourite dress/shirt again? Or you were looking forward to having grandkids or had a particular image of their wedding day? Perhaps you were anticipating the day you'd be checking out hot guys/gals together at the beach, getting your nails done together, or enjoying a fishing trip? Kicking the footy or teaching them your best dance moves?

As you can see, there could be a myriad of thoughts that are leading to your sadness. And of course, this is a tiny list that is likely only the tip of the iceberg, that you may or may not relate to. The truth is that most of these things don't need to be that different and if they are, they may have been, regardless of your child's sexuality or gender identity.

What you'll learn, over time, is that these are all experiences and memories that you were hoping to create with your child and while they may not happen in the way you expected, or they might, you will create new experiences and memories. The sooner you do this work and become more relaxed, open, and comfortable, the sooner you'll be able to experience the joy and new opportunities the two of you and your family can have. This is why it's important to realise you don't have to do this alone, so you can get on that train sooner rather than later.

Unfortunately, in our attempt to 'do the right thing', we can sometimes dismiss, or worse, punish ourselves for our feelings. I hear too often that parents are trying to suppress their feelings in order to be supportive of their LGBTQ+ child. They believe their sadness translates to being an unsupportive parent. Being told that "it's not about you, 'suck it up', put your feelings aside, it's about your child", can also reinforce that sadness is wrong. Once again... It is a process to fully embrace. We need to feel our sadness, we need to grieve. We learn so much more about ourselves as we process the sadness and delve into its origins.

As I've already said, and I will continue to say, it is about you. It is about your child and it's about you. Your feelings do not equal unsupportive or unloving and they do not negate your child's feelings. You can have your feelings and still be supportive of your child. Your words, behaviours, and actions are what will speak to how supportive and loving you are. It's not a competition... Your feelings are yours; it's not even really about your child. This is a journey of personal growth. Even though it may feel excessively painful, we usually evolve into a freer self.

What behaviour tells us

Behaviour demonstrates support and love towards your child, not how you're feeling on the inside. Of course, if you feel you don't love your child, or don't want to be supportive, then that will probably mean your behaviour will reflect that. However, I'm going to assume, because you're here reading this, you do love your child. If you are struggling with your feelings about your child, however, I strongly encourage you to reach out for support.

It is possible you feel you don't love your child... you may have strong negative feelings. This may feel powerful... however, if you historically loved your child, this is likely to be temporary... and even more reason to undergo a formal grieving process to uncover if there is something below the surface fuelling this response. I'm more than happy to support you through this process.

We are complex beings. We can feel a whole range of emotions at one time. This next statement might state the obvious, but here we go. The good news is that this means you can feel sadness and love at the same time. You can feel sadness and still be supportive. You can feel all the feelings you are feeling right now and still love and support your child.

You may need to work on your behaviour, language, and actions if you're struggling on the inside, so you don't project this onto your child. Honouring your feelings is important and needs to be done separately from your interactions with your child.

How do you do this? There are a couple of things to keep in mind. It's important to be honest with yourself. Do the work that you need to do to process your feelings. Including, talking with someone and journaling. Journaling is a great way to begin processing your feelings. You're human and can only suppress those feelings for so long, and the results of that rarely turn out well. You probably already know that and that's why you're reading this. Keep reading, do the activities at the end of each chapter, and reach out for support.

Avoiding feelings never works

The other thing to know is if you try to hide, suppress, or ignore your feelings, your child will probably see right through you. They may not know exactly what you're thinking and feeling, but they will draw their own conclusions, and from my experience, their conclusions are usually worse than the truth. You can tell your child you're finding this difficult, and you are working on it. You don't need to give them the detail, however, it's important they know you're working on it, and you love them, because they will likely be hypervigilant after coming out.

This work that I'm talking about can look a variety of different ways, depending on your personal circumstance. What it isn't is sharing with or burdening your child. That may sound contradictory to previous paragraphs, but bear with me, it will become clear. Talk with someone other than your child, perhaps who's not connected to you or your child, and who's not affected and experiencing their own struggles about your child coming out.

This could be a friend, a family member, or a professional. I have a free guide to help parents find who to talk to on my Instagram bio (at the time of writing). I'd encourage you to take a look, as I go over a variety of important points. Including ensuring that you have explicit consent from your child if you choose anyone other than a professional who's bound by laws and ethics to maintain your and your child's confidentiality. You can also email me or reach out via social media messaging to get a copy.

Balancing honesty

How do you be honest and open with your child without burdening them? The age and maturity of your child is an important element to be taken into consideration here. However, regardless of your child's age, it's not their responsibility to help you work through your struggles and emotions. Especially when it's about them.

So, what do you do? Be honest, without all the details. They're already working through this for themselves, and this is a crucial time for them to know they can count on you. It's also important to note that regardless of your child's age, they will know that something has changed, and that you're struggling in some way. Don't leave them to fill the gaps for themselves. Trust me, it won't be pretty. Share with them a brief statement of how you're feeling and reassure them that this doesn't change the way you feel about them and that you are working through it.

Below is an example of how the conversation might go to get you started.

'Keith, thank you for sharing this with me. I am so glad you did. I will always love you and nothing will change that. You might've noticed that I've been a little {insert emotion or behaviour they may have noticed} lately, but I wanted to let you know I'm talking to someone, and it's not a reflection of how I feel about you. I just need a bit of time to process my feelings and I will always be here for you.'

Guilt and embarrassment

Guilt and embarrassment can come up for a variety of reasons. It may be about one of the following:

- How your feeling

- Your behaviour/responses

The guilt and/or embarrassment can debilitate some parents. I hear it so often. Parents often share, with dread, their regret for how they behaved when their child first shared their news. Their responses vary from a moment of silence to an outright harsh outburst. Regardless, we can all only do the best we can with what we have, at any given moment. Hindsight is a wonderful thing, however, it doesn't help us change the past. We have a choice. We can use it as a learning tool, or we can use it to punish ourselves.

I encourage you to ask yourself is what you feel more helpful in leading you towards being the person and parent you want to be, to behaving in a way that you can be proud of. In the therapeutic approach I use, we don't put the emphasis on whether or not a thought is true, but more on whether it is helpful. Ask yourself, is this way of thinking helpful? If it is, keep it. If it's not, what would be more helpful? Lean into that.

For example, the truth may be that your initial response was not okay. Replaying that message over and over is not helpful for anyone. What is more helpful is to acknowledge your mistake and take action to repair it. We let go of what is not helpful and lean into what is more helpful. (I've shared a simplified version of how we would approach it to assist understanding.)

Guilt or embarrassment can come up for parents who pride themselves in being an open, supportive, progressive individual with LGBTQ+ friends and a tendency to speak up about any wrongdoing. Does this sound like you? Perhaps you're a little surprised about the way you're feeling or reacting to the news of your child's gender identity or sexuality. Has it caught you off guard? This is a common experience for parents.

Sarah

This was Sarah's experience. Her child had come out as gay several years before and she had done her best to be the perfect loving, supportive parent, as had her husband. They welcomed their child's new partners into their lives with loving arms; took part in Pride events, supported other parents, and provided a safe haven for their child's LGBTQ+ friends. They prided themselves in being those parents, the loving, support-ive advocates and allies.

Several years later, their child came out as trans. This was a shock. A bigger shock than the first time. However, they were determined to continue to love and support their child. They did all the same things as they did when their child first came out, but why did this feel so different?

Sarah was reluctant to talk about how she was feeling, but she couldn't shake it off and realised it was affecting her ability to function in life. It had become all-consuming. It took almost 40 minutes for her to muster the courage to share what she was feeling.

She was drowning in shame, guilt, and embarrassment for the struggles she was experiencing about her child coming out as trans. She held so much pride for being a proud, loving, sup-portive, celebratory, rainbow mum that she had been pushing aside the struggles she was feeling about her child's gender identity.

The shock, grief, fear and confusion had caught her by surprise and she had equated those feelings to not being worthy of the 'Rainbow Poster Mum' that she'd felt so much pride in being. She felt like having those feelings translated to not truly loving and supporting her child. She was feeling like a fraud.

The first thing we needed to do was create space for Sarah's feelings. For her to feel safe to feel what she felt and reassured that those feelings did not negate her love and support for her child. What Sarah learned was that trying to push them aside had in fact exacerbated them.

Sarah took a break from the advocacy and pride events to allow herself that space and when she was ready, she returned with a newly found strength within herself and a deeper understanding and connection with her child, herself and her family. She could be there for her husband and other kids, so they could also process how they were feeling, and her advocacy is now stronger than ever. It wasn't easy, however, because she allowed the space for her feelings, it was possible. She worked through the Reconnecting Families Program with me and found herself back in the advocacy seat within a few months.

You're not alone. It's common for parents who have LGBTQ+ friends or other family members, who felt they were open and supportive of the community, to struggle with their own child coming out. It all comes down to our innate feeling of wanting the best for our kids. Wanting them to be safe and to experience a life filled with joy, success, loving relationships, freedom, and ease. And we all know that being LGBTQ+ is not necessarily the easiest or most direct path to that life. It's normal to worry, to feel sad or concerned about your child.

What do you do about this? You continue to love and support your child unconditionally so they have the best chance at the life you wish for them. Kids who are loved and supported unconditionally do much better than those who are not. Your connection with them will be deeper. They will feel safer and more comfortable to confide in you, so you're more likely to hear about their struggles so you can provide the support they need.

Another major cause of guilt and embarrassment is a parent's initial responses and behaviours after a child comes out. As I mentioned above, this can be something subtle or major. If this is you, please understand you can repair it. No matter how poorly you behaved, you can work on repairing the damage to your child and your relationship. This will take time and the amount of time will depend on a variety of factors, such as how poor your response was, how hurt your child was, how your relationship was beforehand and how you go about attempting to repair. You'll learn more about repairing your relationship in chapter eight, however, the important thing to note is that it is possible, so keep reading.

I want you to always remember that no matter what you're feeling; it is not wrong. If you don't feel comfortable, if it's not how you want to feel, you can do something about it. You can work through it. And you don't have to enact your feelings. Protect your child from those feelings while you do your own work and be kind to yourself in the process. Giving yourself a hard time will help no one.

Of course, if you've responded in a way that you're not proud of or that you prefer you didn't, it's to be expected that you will feel some discomfort. However, staying stuck in guilt and regret is unhelpful. They can be part of the grieving process and there may need to be some tears, some journaling and talking to a trusted other, to move through it. Working through this process is important, as remaining caught in it only brings pain and suffering to you and often your loved ones, due to how you respond to your feelings of regret and guilt. I know it's much easier said than done, however, it's time to shift through that guilt and regret. Let it go and take action to move in a direction that feels more in line with how you wish you had responded.

It's time to stop punishing yourself and repair your relationship with your child. Depending on the circumstances, it might be a simple acknowledgement and apology, or it may require something more detailed and complex. Regardless, it is important to ensure it is authentic, that it comes from the heart and that it is not simply to abdicate yourself from guilt because honestly, it won't work. Your child will see straight through you and your subconscious will also not let you off the hook, hence the importance of embracing and working through the grief.

Before you can offer an authentic apology, you need to truly understand what you did wrong, how and why it was hurtful, and you have to truly believe it. Do your research, and learn about why your child might've been upset, however, remember it's not their job to educate you. They've likely shared with you at some stage, therefore spending a bit of time reflecting on conversations that have already happened with them may be helpful to gain some insight.

I ran a 'Release Regret' conversation series in my private Facebook community in 2021, and it was full of powerful reflections, insights, and guidance. The recordings are still there, so I'd encourage you to take a look at those for some insights for yourself. (reach out if you don't know how to find them, I'd be happy to point you in the right direction) In the series, I talk with parents from religious backgrounds who have worked hard to release their regret about how they responded to their child originally. Their response was very much influenced by what they believed in their church. Others spoke about wishing they had more accurate information when their child first came out. And I also spoke to some LGBTQ+ adults who shared their experience of their parents' initial responses and how things had progressed since. Regret and guilt, whilst a normal and often useful response in many facets of our lives, can also be one of the most toxic things we can do to ourselves if we dwell there. For your own health and well-being and that of your loved ones, I encourage you to start the journey of working through and letting go of those feelings. If guilt, regret and lowered mood are something you experience often, I encourage you to seek professional help. You don't need to continue to suffer.

Remember, one wrong turn doesn't stop you from choosing the right turn up ahead.

Worry and Fear

Your child just came out as LGBTQ+ and you're feeling overwhelmed with fear? Fear for them, fear for yourself, fear for your family. Parents want the best for their kids. I know you want your child to be happy, healthy, successful and loved. This new information feels like it has put a shadow on this. There are so many stories and statistics out there about the horrible things that happen to LGBTQ+ people and the struggles they experience, so you're afraid for them. Perfectly understandable, but your worry and fear won't keep them safe, so let's get some perspective and slow that overwhelm with space and work.

Fear and worry can run deep. It can feel like there is no way out, like it's inevitable, given the perceived risks for your child and your family now they're 'out' to the world (or once they come out). Worry and fear can come from all different directions and appear in a variety of shapes and sizes. It's also important to acknowledge that worry is not an emotion. Worry, fear and anxiety go together, but fear is a primal instinct, part of our survival instinct, and worry is the thinking part. We can describe it as unhelpful thoughts about awful things that may happen in the future. Worry fuels fear, though we can also feel fear before we are conscious of any thoughts. Anxiety is the result of ongoing fear and worry. Worrying is both a product and an accelerator of anxiety.

Perhaps you're worried about yourself and how this news will affect the various areas of your life. How it will impact you at work, in your social circles and community groups, and within the extended family.

Does any of this sound familiar?

You have a conservative boss, friend, neighbour, or family member, and are not sure how they'll take it. You don't want to lose that relationship or job or have to have that difficult conversation. Totally understandable. It can be a lot to take in and you've had little time to contemplate it all.

Are you worried about how your other children will take it? How will it affect them and their lives? Will you/they be able to understand? Will it affect them at school or in their workplace and friendship groups? Perhaps they have a friend from a conservative family. How will they take it? Will they treat your child differently?

Are you worried about your child's health, safety, well-being, employment, or relationship future? Afraid of how this will affect their mental, emotional, and physical health, or how they'll manage their sexual health. Whether they will be safe on the streets, on public transport or in nightclubs? How it might impact their education or job prospects or how they might be perceived in their sporting clubs, social circles or other community groups and events. If you remember the horror of the 1980s, you might be worried about your child getting HIV/AIDS.

Before we go any further, I'd like to address concerns about HIV/AIDS, in case I haven't already made it clear. There are many misconceptions about HIV/AIDS, but I feel the most important points for you to understand are:

- HIV/AIDS is not a 'gay' disease. It is a blood born virus that can be transmitted by anyone with the virus, to anyone. It does not discriminate.

- Safe sex practices are important for all sexually active individuals to protect themselves and their intimate partners from HIV/AIDS and other STIs

- There are effective medications to support people living with HIV to live healthy and purposeful lives.

- There are also preventative medications available for those who are at risk.

- Early diagnosis increases the chances of managing HIV effectively

- Removing the stigma around HIV increases the likelihood of regular testing and therefore early diagnosis

- Having open communication about sex, respectful, consensual relationships, and protection, with your child will increase their chances of practising safe sex, testing regularly and accessing preventative medications when needed.

If you and/or your family are people of faith, this can also be a source of significant fear. Worrying if your place of worship and community will accept you and your child? Will they shun you? Will people talk about you? The fear of losing your community that you've dedicated so much of your life to can be scary and it's hard to see beyond. It can feel like you're being made to choose between your faith and your child. It doesn't have to be like that. There are options, though they may not be visible at this moment and may require a lot of work and support.

Many parents I've worked with have worked through these fears and experiences, with varying outcomes. It certainly wasn't easy, though most report it was better than the pain they were in because of the uncertainty and fear. Of course, it looks different for everyone as there are a variety of religions and within each religion, there is also a diverse range of beliefs, values, and responses. This is a complex topic that I don't feel we can do justice to in this book. However, please know that many people have gone through similar to you and made it out the other side. Religion was one topic addressed in several of the 'Release Regret Conversation Series' that you can find in the library in my private Facebook community. Each situation was managed a little differently, so I'd encourage you to watch them if religion and community are a concern for you. There are several books written about religion and sexuality and gender. I have a small list suggested by other parents that I'd be happy to share.

I get it. You've heard the horror stories. But have you heard the success stories? Yes, the statistics about the poor outcomes for LGBTQ+ folk are readily available and it's frightening to think that this might be your child's experience in life. It's heartbreaking that a lot of these things are still a reality, and it's time (beyond time) that it all stops. We all deserve to be safe, happy and loved, and to thrive, exactly as we are.

Did you know, with plenty of love and support, your child can thrive?

It's important to understand that when people are talking about and emphasising the struggles, challenges, and suffering, they're using this data and the stories to advocate for change. They're insisting on safety and love for all, and this is important. You can also be part of the change by being a supportive, loving, and encouraging parent to your LGBTQ+ child.

You have the power to make a significant difference in your child's life and experience in the world. It truly starts at home. So be assured, there is something you can do. A lot, in fact.

It can be difficult, though, if you are coming from a place of fear. That fear can be debilitating. It makes it hard to function in the world and it makes it even harder to be that loving, supportive, encouraging parent that your child needs. It can suck all your attention and energy. Redirecting your attention to love, rather than fear, will help reduce the feelings of over-whelm and enable you to focus more on how you can support your child. I know, I know, easier said than done. Keep reading and reach out for extra support. That's what I'm here for.

Let's look at fear itself. What is it exactly? How does it happen?

The definition of fear, according to the Merriam-Webster dictionary is, "an unpleasant, often strong emotion caused by anticipation or awareness of danger." People fear things or situations that make them feel unsafe or unsure, either physically, emotionally, or psychologically.

Hearing this definition, therefore, makes perfect sense you might be feeling consumed with fear. The danger is not what actually causes fear, it's the anticipation of danger. Fear also stems from feeling unsafe or unsure, either for yourself or a loved one. It's automatic, not a choice... Hence the work.

Safety first

Parents are generally protective of their kids and want the best for them. We tend to be in the habit of anticipating potential danger so we can prevent it from occurring, and keep them safe. We've done it all their lives.

Think about that for a moment. When your child was young, you'd take your child to the playground, and only let them play on the equipment that you felt was age appropriate and safe. You'd take them away from situations that felt unsafe. When adults were having conversations, you felt weren't appropriate for your children's ears, you'd redirect them or the conversation. You'd be mindful to not have chemicals in your child's reach. Get the picture? You've been working hard at keeping your child safe their whole life. Every minute of every day. But also remember that during this time your child has been learning valuable skills and knowledge about keeping themselves safe, too. You've been preparing them for the world around them, a world where you don't have control, so they can live a happy, fulfilled life.

Now is a different scenario. You've just received information about your child that you know can make them more vulnerable. Your desire to protect them doesn't simply go away. The lack of control can exacerbate it because you're feeling less able to protect them. Referring to the part of the definition of fear – "the anticipation or awareness of danger". This may be something you experienced when your child first started school, went on their first date, rode their bike to school for the first time, or caught the bus on their own, or if they're old enough when they started driving a car. You've been here before, however, you could probably anticipate those experiences and this one may have come as a complete surprise, leaving you feeling completely unprepared. It may also surprise you at how primal these feelings are.

Which will you choose?

The unfortunate reality is, we don't live in a perfect world. It's true, there are dangers out there and those dangers are increased for LGBTQ+ people. Of course, it's difficult and perhaps not sensible to ignore those risks, however, it's also not helpful to focus all your attention on them. There are also many incredible people and magical experiences just waiting for your child to take part in. As well as your child's own personal resilience, and ability to make positive choices.... Redirecting more of your attention to those things is much more helpful for your and your child's health and well-being. You have more influence than you think. You have choices and it's up to you to make the ones that serve you and your child best.

You can choose to come from a place of fear. Focus on all that might go wrong. All the risks, the heartbreaking statistics, the chances for hurt or harm for you, your child or other family members.

OR

You can choose to come from a place of love. Focus on all that is right in the world. The growth and development in LGBTQ+ human rights, the positive changes in the laws, and the support that's available in schools and other areas of the community. Your child's strengths and abilities. Their beautiful personality. Every little thing you love about them.

Disclaimer: I understand this is easier said than done, however, I want you to know that it is possible. I'd also like to acknowledge that if worrying seems to be your default, and you consistently worry about many things, it may be worth seeking help to work through this.

Glass half full

This is not a suggestion to ignore the risks or pretend that everything is wonderful. It's placing your day-to-day energy in a place that will serve you and everyone around you much better. When you're able to come from a place of love, you are instilling the same opportunity for your child. You are creating safe, happy, celebratory and joyful experiences for your child. You are supporting them to grow into strong, independent, resilient humans, which will enable them to manage any challenges they face in life more effectively.

In time, you'll be able to use some of that fear, when you're not paralysed by it, to fuel the fire in your belly to advocate for your child and the rights of LGBTQ+ folk. For now though, we're focusing on creating space for you to breathe, to support your child and function in the world without feeling suffocated by the 'what ifs'.

I realise this, like many of my suggestions in this book, is easier said than done, but I want you to know that it is absolutely possible, regardless of how you're feeling at this moment. Many parents I've worked with have felt overwhelmed and often paralysed with fear, among other things, and simply couldn't see a way out until they began this journey with me. Quite quickly, we were able to shine a light on the path ahead, out of the overwhelm, suffering and fear, into joy, peace and love.

Of course, it takes time and commitment to yourself and your child to do the work that is required, but it is entirely possible. And probably more possible than you think. If you're ready to kick that fear out of the park and support your child to be the best they can be, I'd love to support you.

We've spoken about several of the emotions that parents experience when their child comes out and for some time after and I want to acknowledge that not every parent will experience all these, and I have certainly not exhausted the list of emotions that can be experienced. Whatever you're feeling is valid and deserves your kindness and compassion, as well as the space and attention to work through them.

The impacts of external influences

We talked about how your thoughts, beliefs, and values can affect your emotions. I'd now like to spend some time exploring how external influences and environments might affect your thoughts and emotions. In previous chapters, we've also touched on how external environments, situations and experiences can affect your beliefs and values, encouraging you to explore where they came from and whether they actually belong to you. We'll now expand on that a little more.

What are some other external environments and experiences that can impact your emotions in relation to your child's sexuality and gender identity? These influences can come from a variety of places, such as your childhood, parental influences (as a child and/or adult), sporting clubs, friends, extended family, workplace and colleagues, education, social groups and clubs, religion (previously discussed), and let's not forget politics and the media, including advertising, social media, books, journalism and the entertainment industry.

These will all have varying effects on each individual, depending on an array of varying elements, not limited to, personality, exposure levels, including the diversity of exposure, education and level of understanding, access to information, geographical location, family of origin, culture, and types and styles of journalism (accurate or sensationalist).

What's important is for you to realise that these external events impact our self-talk and then how we feel. It's also what and how much you hear from others, what you think others believe or are thinking, what you've been told or overheard in the past, what you read, watch on TV, engage in on social media, what you were exposed to as you're growing up, whether you see LGBTQ+ people in books, movies and TV shows and how they're portrayed and of course the laws and politics in your country, state/province and city. The messaging we receive can range from subtle, right through to quite overt. We can't fool ourselves, though. Regardless of their intensity, they still get through and influence our thoughts, beliefs, and emotions.

Once we realise we're being affected by outside forces, we can make conscious choices about what we do with those. This process is a significant element of the work I do with clients and often makes a world of difference to how they feel within themselves and about their child, not to mention, often a bunch of other areas of their lives. It's like we begin by shining a small flashlight on the topic and it grows into a floodlight, and they can suddenly see things more clearly.

This, of course, will take some time. We're talking about a lifetime of subtle and not-so-subtle messages that deserve the time, attention, kindness and compassion that you would give anyone else who is working through some tough stuff. Trying to rush it will do you no justice, and neither will brushing it under the carpet, or putting it off until another day. Remember, sometimes we do a bit of work, feel lighter, and then need to revisit with greater wisdom.

Understand, for a time you may need to implement some steps that feel difficult, like reducing your time spent with people who are not being helpful in your process, or stop watching your favourite show, because you've realised it's actually homophobic or transphobic, or unfollow some people on social media if their messaging is unhelpful. This doesn't need to be permanent, however, for the short term, while you're working through this process, it is important to do all you can to take care of yourself. You may also find that, as you do this work and look more closely, these actions will be a relief, rather than a burden. Some changes may, however, become permanent because they feel better for you.

Now feels like a good time to remind you of the messages from the parents in my private Facebook community. I asked them, "If you could share one piece of advice or reassurance with other parents, what would it be?" And this was some of their responses:

- Be compassionate towards yourself.

- Work towards understanding the reasons for your choices/behaviours/responses. Even if you've made mistakes, show yourself some kindness.

- Find gratitude for what you did and are doing well.

- Keep perspective on what you're doing well, what you're learning and how you are working towards healing for you, your child and your relationship

- Forgive yourself and allow yourself time.

- These feelings will pass, give yourself some time and space to process your feelings

Read them as many times as you need to and then let's take some action.

MOP ~ Trust your heart and your body

Hold the emotion with love

- Take a deep breath in and exhale – continue deep, slow breaths.

- Notice what emotions you're feeling at this moment – you might say them out loud or inside your head.

- Notice where you're feeling them in your body – your chest, throat, belly, or elsewhere? Simply notice.

- Continue to allow your breath to be deep and slow

- Place your hand or hands on the part of your body where you feel that emotion the strongest.

- Hold your hand/s there and allow your breath to flow to and through that spot.

- Keep your attention on that place, imagine your breath flowing through.

- Allow the exhale to guide your body to release anything that is no longer serving you.

- Allow yourself to sit with this for at least 3 minutes, longer if it feels good for you to do so.

- Once you're ready, gently release your hands and allow your breath to return to its natural state.

Notice what you feel...

If it feels helpful, write it in your journal.

Take Action ~ You've got this!

Gratitude journalling

What is something that brought you joy today? What were your wins?

Gratitude journaling is a wonderful way to encourage your mind to bring more attention to what's going well in your life, rather than what's not.

People have a variety of approaches to this practice. Some write what they're grateful for at the beginning or end of the day, or both. It's also a nice way to connect with family and/or friends, by sharing what you're grateful for at dinner, breakfast, or any other time you gather.

I've made a slight variation to my gratitude practice, and that is, I record 3 wins I had in the day or 3 things I'm grateful for (or a combination of both). This approach feels more accessible to me, particularly if it's been a tough day. I can sometimes find it difficult to think of 3 new things I'm grateful for after a while. I can always recognise my wins for the day, however small.

Let's try it.

Grab your journal/notebook and take a couple of deep breaths. Allow your exhale to guide your body to release any tension.

Gently close your eyes for a moment, so you're not distracted by things you see.

With your eyes closed and your breath relaxed, ask yourself one or all of the following questions and write the first answer that pops into your mind.

What are you grateful for, at this moment?

What brought you joy today?

What were your wins for the day?

Do this three times. (you can ask the same or a different question)

Sit with your answers for a moment. Allow yourself to absorb them.

Key Points

- The roller coaster of emotions, changes and surprises

- Grief – dreams for your child, lost

- Grief – the child you had, gone

- Sadness

- Guilt/embarrassment – about feelings and thoughts

- Guilt embarrassment – about behaviour and responses

- Worry and fear

- The impact of the external environment

Chapter 7

Parent's childhood (young adult) experience

Owning your past to liberate your future

"There are times in our lives when we have to realize our past is precisely what it is, and we cannot change it. But we can change the story we tell ourselves about it, and by doing that, we can change the future."

~ Eleanor Brown ~

Does your child's coming out leave you feeling triggered? Does it bring up emotions, thoughts and feelings related to your own childhood, adolescent, or young adulthood experiences? A trigger is our unconscious mind facilitating a reaction to a situation as a response to experiences. This is often your internal protective mechanism at work, interpreting this situation as similar to a past dangerous, scary, or uncomfortable incident, therefore alerting you of this perceived danger. Keep in mind, triggers can incorrectly alarm us. We're often triggered by emotion rather than an event, so the event can be extremely different. We can't underestimate the impact this can have on our own responses to, and interpretation of, current situations. Much of this impact can lie below our conscious awareness until reactivated by a current experience.

Feeling triggered can be overwhelming and frustrating, especially if you're not clear about what it's about, where it's come from or why you're feeling and reacting the way you are. Something can even trigger us without conscious memories of where they stem from. Those experiences may be way back in your memory and have had no reason to surface until now. This can catch you by surprise. Learning about your triggers, becoming more aware and deepening your understanding will reduce and potentially eliminate fear and doubt, as well as the reactions that go with them. It will enable you to be present with your child's experience and support them in this moment. It will allow you to hear them as they tell you how they're feeling.

The experiences involved in creating triggers stem from what you've experienced as a child, teenager, young adult and into older adulthood, including your experiences parenting your child(ren) throughout their many phases. It also includes your own personal experiences of gender and sexuality, as many of us grew up with a rigid perception of gender that was drummed into us.

As a parent, you have an innate desire and responsibility to protect your child, including sometimes from themselves.

Fears stemming from your earlier experiences can intensify this protective instinct, so it makes sense that you might be feeling sensitive about some of what your child is going through.

Did you experience or witness bullying or other poor behaviour towards or about LGBTQ+ people, as you were growing up? What about people making categorical statements about gender? This, of course, can exacerbate your fears for your own child. Did you go through a stage where you questioned your own sexuality or gender identity, yet concluded that you're straight and cisgender? This can also influence your own understanding of your child's experience. Or perhaps you were a "tomboy" as a child or considered an effeminate male and feel that this is the same thing for your child.

All these experiences may increase your fear and worry and create or intensify doubt. But hopefully, it will also allow you the opportunity for a deeper insight into your child's experience. While the experience of being a tomboy or effeminate male is different to being gender diverse, as one is about behaviour and the other is about our sense of self, there's likely to be some crossover in how we're perceived in the world.

Before we go any further, I'd like to invite you to consider the possibility that while your response to your child may result from being triggered by past experiences, it may also result from previously unexamined beliefs about this topic. Or both?

Keep in mind, our reactions and behaviours are not just a result of being triggered. You might remember from Chapter 4, they also derive from our own beliefs, some of which are created by traumatic experiences, like bullying. The values, beliefs, and opinions of those around us when growing up created others, as well as other influences such as the books we read, the TV we watched or the talk-back radio we listened to. It may be difficult to tell the difference. Hearing about your child's sexuality or gender identity might have triggered uncomfortable feelings within you and it may be hard to tell where that has come from, past experiences or unexamined beliefs. Remember, those beliefs may trigger these feelings.

Unpacking and unlearning your past

A variety of things trigger human beings, from past experiences. These can range from subtle, not having a tremendous impact on our lives, to massive, causing significant pain and suffering. Present experiences can cause reactions within us that can sometimes feel uncomfortable. Our reactions may surprise us and leave us wondering where the feelings and/or reactions are coming from. Other times we can be quite aware.

These triggers can originate from our experiences relating to our parents, siblings, other family members, school and other friends and peers, amongst other things. We react to our triggers and can be at risk of projecting our fears onto our children, trying to protect them from the same experiences. Therefore, it makes sense that what you've experienced and witnessed in your life would impact how you react to your child coming out.

Allowing yourself to feel what you feel with kindness and compassion is the best way to learn more about your triggers and reflect on whether they are in fact triggers or unexamined beliefs. Taking away the judgement and criticism and approaching them from a curious, observational perspective will begin the process of releasing them. The first step is awareness, becoming more aware that they exist, what they are and how they feel. You may not have clear memories from your childhood, but you may have an awareness of a vibe or type of behaviour in particular environments. Depending on your experience you may not begin with compassion... and that's okay. Allow the process, acknowledging all your emotions, including anger. Let your personal journey be yours, ensuring it does not impact your child.

What triggers you? Start with the easy ones. The ones that you can clearly identify and work your way through to the more subtle ones. It's important not to ignore the subtle ones as they're often the bigger culprit. There's an activity at the end of this chapter to assist you through this process. Let's explore possibilities together.

Examples of experiences that might trigger your fear, worry or other unpleasant feelings:

- Experiencing bullying or other types of abuse

- Witnessing bullying of others who are or are presumed to be LGBTQ+.

- Hearing adults in your life talk negatively or harshly about LGBTQ+ people.

- Feeling like you were/are a tomboy or effeminate male and experiencing unpleasant reactions, behaviours or comments towards you.

- Living in an environment that wasn't accepting of difference.

- Growing up in a conservative environment with rigid ideas about how the world should be.

- Identifying as LGBTQ+ and having unpleasant experiences. (If this is your experience it might be a good idea to consider professional support to work through it to ensure you process it rather than continue to be re-triggered. That is have a safe place to land.)

These are a few of the common experiences people I work with have shared that lead to them feeling triggered by their child coming out. The degree of impact and time it takes to process and heal these experiences vary depending on the severity and personal impact it has had. For some people, it's possible to work through this on their own and for others they require assistance. Though what is true for all people is that the process is quicker when done with adequate, effective support.

It's important to know that as well as being triggered, some of these experiences are also likely to influence your opinions and beliefs about gender and sexuality, impacting your reactions and feelings about your child coming out. This may require a process of unpacking, unlearning, and relearning, which will be best done with the support of an experienced professional, as we all have considerable blind spots to how our experiences influence our behaviour.

We can categorise internal responses or reactions to these experiences in several areas. Fear, doubt or not trusting your child's understanding of themselves, perhaps questioning if it's a phase and feeling like your beliefs and values are being challenged. To expand on what we've already discussed, earlier in this book, it's important to understand when, why and how you're being triggered and/or influenced by learned opinions or beliefs. This could be easier said than done, as it's also possible that it may be different to what you originally thought it was. There may be deeper events that trigger the trigger.

Triggering fear

As we know, there are many life experiences that might cause you to have a fearful or worried response about your child's future.

What's important to remember is that we live in a different time. There's still a lot of work to do and the level of risk will vary depending on where your child lives and spends their time. Your behaviours and responses have an incredible amount of power, though. You can make a significant difference to the way your child experiences the world. When they have a safe, loving, supportive environment to come home to, a place where they can comfortably express themselves, they'll be much better placed to manage the struggles they face in society. The most common factor for children to develop resilience is at least one stable, committed, loving relationship with a supportive parent, caregiver or other adult.

You can also, when you're ready, start to have your own impact on society's understanding of and behaviour towards the LGBTQ+ community. Kids are not born discriminatory; it's learned behaviour. It comes from what they see and hear from the adults in their lives. The media, including social media, and poorly behaved people they're exposed to. That means we can make a difference with education and accurate information.

This is exactly why Pride parades and other events are so important. They create visibility, raise awareness, and show the importance of love, compassion, kindness and celebrating all humans. But I digress. Children are okay with difference and if they're well informed, with good role models and supported to create an open, understanding, and compassionate approach to life, rather than taught cruelty, they will grow into beautiful adults who help to create a beautifully celebrated, diverse community.

We previously recognised that fear is also a significant influencer in creating a sense of disbelief or not trusting your child's ability to know what they're feeling and experiencing. As mentioned in Chapter 5, questioning whether it's a phase is one of the most common responses, I hear. Remember, it's important to believe what your child's telling you about how they feel and support them. Life is all about phases and stages, they're valid, and your child requires your love and support.

The unfortunate and unintended outcome of this 'it's a phase' response is that your child will feel like their feelings and experiences are being dismissed. This is hurtful and upsetting and may cause your child to withdraw and not trust you to confide in. Bringing us to the next point, it'll make it even harder to protect them.

The overwhelming urge to protect

I totally understand this overwhelming urge to protect your children. I am also very aware that this feeling doesn't disappear as they grow into adults (sorry to disappoint you), it simply changes. In fact, in some situations, it can feel even more challenging, as when they're teenagers and adults you have less and less influence.

If you can increase your awareness of the causes of these fears and other instigators, it'll give you the best chance of working through them, so they no longer take over your life.

I'd like to introduce you to Sally. Her experience serves as a compelling illustration of how a parent's intense desire to safeguard their child can often lead to increased anxiety and stress. However, by acknowledging and exploring the emotions evoked by experiences and unexamined beliefs, one can effectively ease the overwhelming feelings.

Sally & Jay

I remember when I first met Sally. She was a single mother with 3 kids. Her middle child, Jay came out as trans when they were 14. Sally shared that her child was assigned female at birth but had told her recently that they're a boy and requested she use a new name and he/him/his pronouns. Jay had always been interested in stereotypically male things. He played footy with the boys at lunch and recess, he demanded cars and trucks as birthday gifts from a young age and was always out playing the 'rough and tumble' games with his brother and his friends. He refused to wear skirts and dresses and was constantly asking to have his hair cut short. Sally could totally relate.

Sally thought Jay was a tomboy, just like she was when she was growing up. This was a fair assumption. Your interests, likes and dislikes, and the length of your hair don't determine your gender. Not every child who behaves similarly to Jay will be trans, however in this case, Jay is. This was difficult for Sally however the biggest struggle she had was the fear that this would pass, as it did for her, and in the meantime, Jay would make some decisions that would have a negative impact on his life.

In this situation, Sally was clear that her own experiences of being a tomboy as a child, and how she was perceived and treated were triggering her fear and concerns. She was struggling to understand how this was different for her child. Full of fear and worry, Sally asked, "Isn't she just a tomboy, like I was? Won't she grow out of it, like I did? And then what? What if she's changed her body in a way that she regrets?" All fair concerns.

Her own personal experience was having a tremendous impact on her ability to listen and understand what Jay was expressing to her. She could see so much of herself in him. The question here was whether Sally was actually being triggered, or if she was letting her own beliefs from her personal experience cloud her ability to truly hear what Jay was saying and believe what he was feeling. It was possibly a combination of the two.

Regardless, Sally could not truly hear Jay. Her reactions and responses were solely based on her own experiences. She was constantly trying to convince Jay that he would grow out of it and one day grow up to be a beautiful, happy, successful woman. This response only alienated Jay more and more. After some time, they couldn't be in the same room together without snapping or arguing with each other. Sally was feeling frustrated, confused, scared, and sad. All she wanted to do, was protect her child from making, what she believed to be, a big mistake that could have lifelong consequences. Understandable, right?!

Jay eventually shut down completely and refused to be in shared spaces with the rest of the family. He spent as much time as possible out of the house, and when he was home, he spent all his time in his bedroom. Sally was concerned and didn't know what to do, or which way to turn. When the school made contact, also concerned about how much Jay had withdrawn, Sally decided enough was enough. She had tried giving Jay space, confronting him, and a bunch of 'offering an olive branch' approaches. None of them worked. She was only met with more resistance and withdrawal.

Thankfully, Jay's school knew about my services and shared my details with Sally. She emailed me soon after her conversation with the school. At this point, she was desperate. She shared she was really concerned for Jay's well-being, her family, and "to be honest", she said, "I don't know how much more I can take". The best approach was to arrange a phone call for a brief chat, where I shared with Sally that Jay might be more upset about the gender conversation than she realised.

Sally felt like she'd tried everything. The one thing though, she hadn't tried and did not know how much impact it was having, was to trust Jay. To believe in what he was telling her about how he was feeling. After the initial conversations about Jay's gender, when Sally had been clear that she felt like this was the same as how she felt as a teenager, they hadn't returned to the conversation. At that moment, Sally believed she was being helpful and reassuring Jay. She thought she was doing the right thing by not speaking about it anymore because Jay had made it clear he wasn't interested.

The problem was, Jay was feeling dismissed and isolated. The consequence of this was that Jay no longer wanted to share his feelings or hear what Sally had to say. He'd decided it was safer to not talk at all. Of course, this was not good for anyone, especially Jay's mental and emotional well-being.

It's a simple mistake to make. In trying to protect her child, she hadn't realised she'd caused him to withdraw. She wasn't aware that her disbelief and attempt to protect him was the cause of Jay's behaviour change, because she thought it was just a phase he was going through. Sally had thought something else was going on. She had put it down to a combination of hormones, 'normal teenage behaviour', and other things she imagined could be going on. Her mind had run wild on her. She was concerned about drugs, bullying, struggles with schoolwork, friendship problems, and perhaps even boyfriend troubles. All valid and reasonable concerns. Jay refused to talk, so Sally continued to fill in the gaps herself and worry about all the possibilities.

During our early conversations, with the gift of hindsight and some breathing space, Sally could reflect on how upset Jay had been directly after that initial conversation and that in every conversation after that, Jay was trying to convince Sally that he was trans. Sally continued to brush it off as simply being a tomboy, just like her.

After some time and space to work through her own triggers and fears, Sally learned the best thing for her to do in that moment, was to provide a safe, supportive environment for Jay to work through his feelings and experiences.

Creating this space for your child will allow them to work through all their feelings, explore their options and deepen their understanding of themselves. As a parent, I recently spoke with articulated beautifully.

This parent has a trans child and another child who recently came out as bisexual. She shared, "My daughter is the only person who can know how she feels. I have to trust this, regardless of my own thoughts and feelings, and be there for her if she wants to talk about it."

Taking this approach means that if your doubts, disbelief, or fears, turn out to be correct, they'll be more able to come to you and share their feelings. Alternatively, if your child is stuck in, the 'I have to convince you' mode, their ability to explore and learn about themselves will be hindered.

That initial conversation with Sally was the beginning of a beautiful, healing, growth and reconnection journey for her, Jay, and their family, which I had the privilege of walking alongside them and witnessing. You'll hear more about Sally and Jay a little later, but for now, Sally could now realise that her own experiences had impacted her ability to hear and understand Jay's experiences and feelings, openly. It wasn't long before Jay was spending less time in their bedroom and more time with the family and Sally felt like she could breathe for the first time in a long time.

Unconditional love and support

The best way to protect your child is to LASU them. (Love And Support Unconditionally) Reading this book, and doing this work on yourself is a big step in the right direction. By addressing and overcoming your own fears and ensuring that you don't project them onto your child, you can discover effective strategies to manage your struggles and triggers. It is also important to examine and dismantle any unhelpful beliefs that may hold you back. This process will allow you to show up more authentically for your child, providing them with the love and support they need. This will place them in the best possible position to manage any struggles that might come their way, throughout their life.

MOP ~ Trust your heart and your body

Notice 5 things

This is a common grounding and centring exercise. People use it to ease anxiety, help them be more present, slow a racing mind and generally calm the system.

Where ever you are right now, notice:

- 5 things you can **see** (2 far away, 2 medium distance, one close up) Pay attention to the whole object, then bring your attention to the details you can notice.

- 4 things you can **feel** (what you can feel on your skin – your clothes, watch, something in your hand, glasses on your face etc)

- 3 things you can **hear**.

- 2 things you can **smell**.

- 1 thing you can **taste**.

Note: if you have any challenges with any of the senses, simply do the ones you have easy access to.

Notice what you feel...

If it feels helpful, write it in your journal.

Take Action ~ You've got this!

Reflection time

This activity is a guide to self-reflection.

The goal is to become more aware of what is influencing your reactions towards your child coming out. Once you have increased awareness and understanding, you'll be more able to work towards releasing the fear and overwhelm.

Begin by writing all experiences you feel may have contributed to your reactions about your child coming out. Like other activities, write without filter, judgement, or criticism. It might surprise you what comes up.

This could be behaviour you witnessed in the schoolyard, your family home, family gatherings or in other social situations.

It may be outright homophobic and/or transphobic behaviours and comments, or more subtle indications of intolerance or disapproval.

It might be your own personal experiences of how you felt and/or were treated.

It may even be a sense of disregard or disapproval of any difference at all.

Like other writing activities, once you feel you're finished, ask yourself, "And what else?"

Once complete, you can use this information to inform your next steps.

Can this information help you differentiate between your experiences and your child's?

Can this differentiation help you shift towards hearing your child more clearly?

Are you able to recognise which are triggers and which are unexamined beliefs that may require some unlearning?

Could you benefit from some professional support to work through these further?

Sometimes our most important learning is that we can't and don't need to do things alone. Seeking support can be one of the most rational, productive, and effective actions we can take.

Self-reflection can be challenging. If this activity felt tough, return to a MOP, either in this chapter or any others that have felt helpful.

Key Points

- Your past experiences impact your present.

- Those experiences, can create unhelpful beliefs and trigger fear and other powerful emotions when your child comes out.

- Your desire to protect your child might get in the way of you hearing, seeing, and trusting them

- Notice, recognise, acknowledge, and work through your triggers and unexamined beliefs

- Create a safe, supportive environment for your child to figure things out for themselves, while you walk alongside them

Chapter 8

Repair

It's not too late to make it right

"Don't carry your mistakes around with you, place them on the floor and use them as steppingstones to where you want to go"

~ Karon Waddell ~

You're reading this book because you want to improve your relationship with your LGBTQ+ child. This could be because you responded in ways that you feel damaged the relationship and it needs repairing, or you're looking to improve and grow the relationship, or you want some assurance that you're on the right track. We're going to dive deep into what that can look like. For some of you that will feel almost impossible and for others you might feel like the word repair seems a little much, like the relationship is ok and doesn't require repair. If the latter is you, consider this an opportunity to build a deeper relationship with your child. Who doesn't want a deeper connection with their child?

If you relate more to the former, I want to assure you that yes, you can repair your relationship. I am yet to meet an LGBTQ+ person who, given the chance, wouldn't want to have their relationship with their parents repaired. When they indicate they don't, it is usually because they can't imagine it being possible. They can't see how their parents would change their opinions and behaviours. When asked if there was a magic wand and if their parents were able to respond in a way that felt good to them, they said that would be their preference. (Disclaimer: I have not met every LGBTQ+ person and had this conversation, so I'm sure there are some that would say no thank you, but that doesn't have to be your child)

So, yes, there is hope. You can repair and/or grow your relationship with your child. For this to happen, you need to be prepared to dig deep, do the work, and be open to learning. You've got this! I'd love to walk this journey with you. Shine a light on your heart and what you know to be true. You love your child and want the best for them and your relationship with them.

What's gone wrong?

Let's look at some areas where things can go wrong and how they could go better.

Do you feel you messed up or made some mistakes when they came out? Did you do okay when they came out but messed up since? Or maybe you've 'got it wrong' from the start. Is your child trans and you keep making mistakes with their pronouns or new name? Are you reluctant to engage with their new partner, or simply behaving differently towards them than you do their sibling's (opposite gender) partner? Do you find yourself constantly in some form of conflict with your child about anything to do with gender or sexuality, or maybe anything at all? Do you feel like they're just wanting to argue for the sake of it? Or maybe you feel you can't get anything right with them, you keep putting your foot in it, resulting in a constant feeling of walking on eggshells. Or perhaps these things happened in the past and you haven't spoken in a long time and do not know how to reconnect.

I know, thinking about this feels uncomfortable, it's not an easy topic to broach, but fighting with your child, or feeling distant or disconnected from them, is pretty uncomfortable too, right? While you read through this chapter take extra special care of yourself. Make yourself a cup of tea or other beverage of choice, get comfortable, create some time and space so you can truly feel what you feel and be kind to yourself. Understand that while this might be tough, on the other side it will be much more pleasant than you are already experiencing, and I'm here for you. We've been together for seven chapters now and hopefully, you're feeling like you can trust the processes and yourself enough to dive deep into this.

Messed up – part one – at the time your child came out to you

Let's begin with 'maybe you could've done better' when your child came out. There are so many variations to this, different ways it might look. What is your version? Do you believe you messed up? Or is your child telling you or hinting at you that you could have done better? Regardless, the approach can be the same or similar.

Before you read any further, take a moment to reflect on your response/s and reaction/s to your child when they came out. Also, include any reactions you shared with others that your child may be privy to. Be honest with yourself. We'll go into this a little deeper at the end of the chapter, however for now, I'm inviting you to recall the experience, and maybe write it down, so you have an accurate reflection of this as you read on.

How do you feel you messed up? Were you so shocked and overwhelmed that you didn't hide your anger or distress? Were you trying to keep it together, but your distress and concern were obvious? Or did you believe you were effective in hiding your shock, but your child just knew?

Consider that regardless of what you think about your response, your child may feel differently. If you feel like your child is overreacting or being unreasonable, it is possible that they experienced your response differently from how you intended or perceived it, and they may be feeling hurt. Remember, your child has been reading your reactions since birth. Looking back, in hindsight, you may see your behaviour in a different light. Maybe now, with time and the opportunity of sitting with your cuppa, you may see your child's perspective a little better.

We'll begin with the more subtle reactions and work our way to the more overt. Please remember to steer away from judgement, that is judgement on yourself or others who may have reacted differently than you. At the end of the day, we're all here for the same reasons and that is to rebuild, repair and reconnect with your kids. You can't change the past, however, you can have a significant impact on the present and future.

Let's explore this together. I understand this may be tough to do, it may feel uncomfortable, challenging, and/or confronting, however, it is necessary and will ease the existing discomfort. I know, I've said this before, and I'll no doubt say it again... Do your best to be gentle with yourself and remember to ask for support if you need it.

Which of the following relates most closely to your experience?

Mild or subtle responses.

These can be small comments, facial expressions, body language, a roll of the eyes, or perhaps the omittance of supportive words or comments. You may or may not be aware that you have done anything to upset your child. It may only be because they told you that you are even aware of them being upset with you. You may not agree with them or be able to see from their perspective, yet. Another reminder, they know you really well and have been hyper-vigilantly assessing your responses for years, if not decades.

Mediocre responses

These might include some of the above, with extra comments added. Some comments I've heard parents regretting or LGBTQ+ people being upset about are things like:

It's just a phase.

You're too young to know.

You're just copying xxx, I want you to stop spending so much time with them.

Don't be so ridiculous, you can't be because...

We can fix this, don't worry, we'll get you a therapist, take you to church...

You're just upset because your breakup with xxx was so awful.

Stronger, more overt responses

Any of the above with additional hurtful comments about LGBTQ+ folk. Threats to disown or kick your child out of the house and/or family. Strong language against LGBTQ+ people, their expressions, and their behaviours.

Regardless of which category you fall into, there is hope, that you can repair the damage. I don't need to tell you that the more severe your response, the more work you may be required to do, however, it is definitely possible, and I am feeling grateful you've chosen me and my book to guide you. Remember, you can choose more in-depth guidance and support via my website.

Sometimes, the more subtle, the harder it is to identify the error or the inner prejudices. If you were more extreme in your response, your child may be more grateful and open to the obvious attempts to take responsibility.

Keep in mind, all of this also depends on the relationship you had with your child prior to them coming out.

Messed up – part two – since your child came out

The time your child invites you into their world is not the only time parents mess up. Even when everything seemed okay at first, many families experience episodes scattered throughout other times. There's so much to learn, leaving many opportunities for mistakes and you certainly wouldn't be alone in that one either.

Messing up later can also look a variety of different ways. It may be subtle, overt, or anywhere in between. You may be conscious of it, or your child may let you know. Some examples of this could be:

- Using incorrect pronouns or names

- Calling their partner, a friend

- Talking or behaving in a way that implies their identity is temporary.

- Being over the top with their friends or partner (appearing to cover up hidden feelings)

- Treating their partner differently from other sibling's

partners

- Making mistakes with friends' or partner's pronouns or names

- Avoiding conversations about sexuality or gender identity

- Making excuses for others' poor behaviour and mistakes

- Continuing to hide the truth from others.

- Outing them without their consent.

- Not making allowances for gender-affirming needs e.g. clothing, medical care, hairstyling, etc.

They're not trying to upset you

You may feel like they're being too sensitive, impatient, or simply trying to pick a fight.

I want to reassure you that this is unlikely to be the case. Your child is not just trying to be difficult. They're trying to navigate a complex world in the best way they can. Just like you. Something else to consider is that if they're a child, adolescent, or young adult their brains have not fully developed, therefore they're less able to regulate their emotions. If you don't believe me and still think they're just trying to be difficult, I invite you to take a moment to consider the hours, days, weeks and maybe even years, they have been preparing themselves to come out, to you and the rest of the world. They may have been armouring themselves for the responses, anticipating or expecting rejection, hence they'll be a little hyped up.

Let's explore this in a bit more depth. They're finding their voice, creating spaces where they can be their authentic selves and fighting for safety and comfort in those spaces. There's often a lack of those spaces, especially in the early days, therefore home and family are even more important.

I'm sure you'd agree with me we all want to and deserve to feel safe, loved, and comfortable in our own homes and within our families. When there are mistakes made or unhelpful comments made within those environments, it becomes harder for your child to manage the outside world. It can also result in them coming across as intolerant, impatient, or cranky. While it might feel like they are being picky to you, for them they're likely thinking something like, "Can't I just relax at home and not have to put up with those comments, looks and/or mistakes?"

I hear you. You'd like the same. You're feeling like you're walking on eggshells, that each time you open your mouth you don't know if you'll be ignored, grunted at, or worse, verbally attacked.

I meant what I said. Everyone deserves to feel safe, comfortable, loved and relaxed in their home and family. It is tough to live in a house or share space with someone who regularly appears angry, sad, reactive and/or defensive. The difference is that your child, like many LGBTQ+ peoples, may not feel safe outside of the home and family, therefore they are looking for some respite, space to breathe.

What can you do to create that space where you can all feel relaxed, comfortable, safe, and loved in the family home? Improving communication is vital for repairing and creating healthy relationships. Active, non-defensive listening is an effective strategy for developing authentic, intentional communication within your family. Let's explore what that is and how to do it, a little more.

Undistracted listening

We all want to be heard and understood, however, that's often easier said than done, particularly with all the distractions we have in today's world. I'm sure you've had enough social experiences to realise that there's a significant distinction between someone listening and being heard. Have you ever had an experience where the person you're talking to doesn't seem like they're quite there with you, or they're just not quite getting what you're saying?

I think we've all been there, and I'm sure we can agree, it doesn't feel very good. Whether they're distracted by their phone, other people or something else, it feels unpleasant, to say the least, and the more important we feel what we're saying is, the more upsetting or annoying, it can feel.

Studies have shown that often, people who should be listening are instead, distracted. This can happen at varying levels, and while it is not a new concept, our mobile phones are definitely adding to the situation.

I read an article a while ago (unfortunately I can't remember the source), stating that we're distracted by our mobile phones, even when they're on silent. While we could all do with some improvements in our mobile/cell phone etiquette, did you know that the soft buzz from 'vibration mode' is enough to draw your attention away from your conversation, even if you don't answer or look at it? It certainly surprised me at the time that I read this, however, I have since paid more attention and realised it is true. If my, or anyone else's phone buzzes, I'm immediately distracted, even if only for a second. How distracted depends on my current circumstances, however, it certainly creates a break in my focus.

Sometimes it'll trigger me to get lost in my own thoughts, while others it creates a subtle break, where the flow of my conversation is then affected, sometimes mildly and other times, significantly. My solution to this is to put my phone on 'Do not disturb', if I'm having an important conversation and to put my phone away when I'm with others. Do I do this all the time? No, I certainly have a long way to go in the world of minimising the distractions from my phone, however, I'm working on it and I invite you to do the same.

We can't blame it all on technology.

Studies have shown that not only are we constantly distracted by our devices, but our attention span is also shrinking, however, we can't blame it all on technology. It might surprise you to hear that one of our most common distractions is our own mind. It's true. Depending on who you listen to, we have somewhere between 6,000 and 50,000 thoughts a day. Any wonder we're frequently distracted by our own minds.

Next time you're having a conversation with someone, notice what your mind is doing. There's a good chance you'll be thinking about the next thing you need to do, what's for dinner, admiring their new shoes, wondering who cuts their hair, telling yourself a story about what they're saying, or simply planning your response.

Does any of this sound familiar?

Now think about when you are the person wanting to be heard. You can usually tell when that person isn't really with you, can't you? And then you're distracted and considering all the reasons they're not really listening.

Perhaps the story you're telling yourself is that they don't care, they're not interested in what you're saying, they think you're 'stupid', what you're saying isn't important, they don't believe you or they like the other person/people in the room more than you.

Result: you feel unimportant, not valued, supported, or cared about. Just to name a few.

AND the more important the conversation is to you, the more hurt, frustrated, upset, or angry you may feel.

Non-defensive listening

We can also get distracted by our emotions, thoughts, and feelings. Practising non-defensive listening can help us to not react in an unhelpful way. When we're listening defensively, it means we're not really focused on what's being said, the intent of the other person, or their feelings and needs. We are more focused on how to protect ourselves, prove ourselves right or argue our point. This means our response will be more likely to be reactive and unhelpful.

When what we're hearing is difficult to hear, it's challenging to stay out of that defensive mindset.

Strategies that can be helpful are to stay out of, or recover from defensiveness:

- Be mindful of love and respect.

- Stay in touch with your love for the person and less focus on their behaviour.

- Breathe! Now's a good time to practice a gentle extend-ed exhale. (try not to be too obvious with this one as it might sound like a sigh)

- Avoid taking the other person's comment personally.

- Ask for clarity.

- Push the pause button. Let the other person know you need to take a moment.

Active, non-defensive listening

What can we do to make a difference in our conversations?

Great question! Remember, you can't control what others do or don't do, but you can alter your own behaviour. You can practice active, non-defensive listening strategies which will allow you to truly hear the other person, connect with them on a deeper level and learn and understand more about their experiences. A side note, this is not limited to your relationship with your child. Bonus, you can practice this in every single conversation you have, with anyone. You'll also be role-modelling behaviours that are more conducive to deeper connections, within your circle of people. The more you do it, the easier it will be with your child.

Active, non-defensive listening is a great way to create deep, meaningful conversations. It helps keep you focused and attentive during a conversation and avoids defensiveness. With your kids, it will assist you to truly hear what they're telling you and reduce the risk of misunderstandings and arguments.

Try some of these examples out in your next conversation:

Listen with an open mind and heart, without trying to defend yourself, your opinions, or your beliefs. I know, I know, easier said than done, but remember this is a work in progress, and you won't always succeed. Simply do your best.

- Stop talking...

- Avoid interruption!

- Maintain eye contact — that doesn't mean your eyes are glued to theirs, that could get creepy.

- Use engaging body language and facial expressions — open, nodding the head, face them, facial expressions reflective of the context of the conversation. Avoid folding your arms.

- Show interest and understanding.

- Ask questions, when appropriate, to clarify anything you don't understand and show interest and curiosity in what they're telling you.

- 'Summarise' what you heard to clarify you've understood correctly.

- Do NOT look at your phone. Understanding that looking at your phone can be a defence mechanism... If you need a break, take a toilet break and a few deep breaths.

- Avoid planning your response. You'll be surprised, when you're actively listening, your response will come a lot easier and won't need so much planning. This is because you've properly heard and understood the other person. If you need to take a bit of time to consider your response, this is also okay and much more appreciated when you've been actively listening.

- Avoid the need to be right. When we get caught in the space of needing to be right, it is impossible to listen well. We are more focused on how to prove ourselves right, defend ourselves and dismiss the other person's perspective.

When you want to be heard

There are at least two sides to most conversations and as important as it is for you to actively, non-defensively listen, it's as important for you to be heard. Not everyone in your life will have had this mini lesson on active listening, so what can you do for yourself, to feel more heard?

You can begin by letting the other person know that what you have to say is important, and it's important to you that they listen, without distraction, to what you have to say. A caveat to this is to be careful how you say it, as when we lead a conversation this way the other person can worry, particularly if they're your child. The mind can run away from them, concerned they're in trouble or something is wrong, something serious. It is, however, a great opportunity to role model effective communication skills, sharing with them what you need in order to feel heard.

If need be, you can let them know you feel like they're distracted and check in if they're ok, if now is a good time to have the conversation, or if it will be better to continue the conversation at another time. Most of the time people don't realise they're distracted, until after the fact and therefore a polite, gentle prompt can be helpful. It's important not to make them wrong. It could make a difficult situation worse. This can be the case, especially if this is a new style of communication for all of you.

Practising and role modelling effective, respectful, wholehearted communication is one of the most important gifts parents can give to their children, though of course, not limited to the parent/child relationship.

This experience can be quite different for everyone and will probably take time and practice. The key thing to remember is to remove distractions and be as present as possible to the person who is talking to you. Be kind to yourself and understanding of others. Practice open, honest, and curious communication...

The importance of language

Talking about communication, language can be quite powerful. That old saying, "Sticks and stones may break my bones, but names will never hurt me", is not true. In fact, words can be very harmful. If we're all honest, we can probably identify a time or times when something that was said to us hurt us. There's plenty of evidence to say that psychological and emotional abuse or torment can be more painful and difficult to heal. I believe that saying was a strategy used to take the power out of a bully's words, which is helpful in some ways and, we now know better than to dismiss words as harmless. We know words can be powerful in a variety of ways, so it's important that we choose them carefully, followed by actions that accurately reflect those words. Especially when we're communicating with someone who might be feeling sensitive or vulnerable to a particular topic.

This leads me to explore the language that you use when talking to and about your child. That can be whether you avoid mentioning their partner's name, whether you'll use the words, gay, trans, LGBTQ+, or whether you avoid the topic altogether or have obvious gaps and/or hesitation in your conversations. It might be telling untruths to avoid acknowledging your child's sexuality or gender identity. An example of this might be when your neighbour asks if your daughter has a boyfriend, and you respond by saying, "No, she's not interested in dating as she's focused on her studies right now". When in fact, she has a girlfriend.

Now of course it's not necessarily your neighbour's business, and you may not want to have the conversation with them regardless of your child's sexuality, this, of course, would depend on the type of relationship you have with your neighbour. You may also suspect or fear they're homophobic. There are many things to take into consideration, including whether your child is okay with being out to the neighbour. In this scenario, however, if your child is out and happy for the neighbour to know, yet you avoid it by either diverting the conversation or telling a white lie, this can send a message to your child that you are embarrassed or ashamed of them.

It may be true. You may feel some embarrassment or shame and as we've discussed earlier, this is a normal part of the process. What's important here is that you're honest with yourself and do the work to move through that shame and embarrassment. If your child hears you, or is made aware, explain to your child that you're aware this might be difficult for them and for now, you're needing a bit of time to process things for yourself, before having the conversations with others. Let them know you're working on it, perhaps even share how and that you will do your best to get to a place where you can feel more comfortable being open. Also, be aware that while it's not okay to ask your child to lie or project your own shame onto them, you can ask them for a bit of time.

There are many variations to this scenario and while it is perfectly normal to struggle, it's also normal for your child to be frustrated, upset and potentially angry about it. This is the reason I work closely with parents to address these feelings and find strategies to not only manage them but also find ways to create open, safe communication with their child to ascertain mutually agreeable and acceptable compromises and adaptations.

Pronouns – the struggles to get them right

Pronouns and name changes can be the source of a lot of struggles, pain, and conflict within families. It's hard to remember to use different names and pronouns when you've known the person as something else for their entire life. It's even harder when you don't understand why they're doing it or are in disbelief. If you've arrived at this point in this book and are still struggling to understand, I encourage you to seek extra support. One-to-one, therapeutic support is a completely different experience from simply reading words on a page. It'll surprise you how much difference it can make. It's okay to make mistakes, however, while ever you're struggling and therefore using the old name and pronouns regularly, there'll be tension between you and your child, you'll remain in conflict, or worse, become alienated from them. And neither of us want that for you, or them.

As a side note, what I've found, is that parents often prioritise paying for their kids' therapy over accessing support for themselves, believing they need the help more or it's more important for them to get the support. This is very noble however; the truth is what they need is for you to be okay. They need you to understand them, to love them and support them, unconditionally and to get to a place where their sexuality or gender identity is no longer an issue in your family. Of course, if your child has mental health concerns, absolutely seek support for them. But also, don't underestimate the impact that accessing external support for yourself will have on, not only your LGBTQ+ child but on your whole family.

One of the most common questions I get asked from support-ive parents of trans kids is "How do I stop messing up? I can't seem to remember their pronouns or new name. I try, but I'm just so used to their old one. I've been using that for x number of years. It's hard to change." This is true. It is hard to change. Habits are hard to break. I won't deny that. I too have made mistakes using the wrong name or pronoun for someone.

The simple answer to these questions is, to take responsibility, practice using the correct pronoun and make a commitment to yourself and your child to stop making mistakes. Do the work and be kind to yourself in the process. Also, understand that taking responsibility is different to blaming. Active pos-itive reinforcement like practice and reward is much more effective than self-punishment and self-recrimination... i.e. "You idiot, you did it again..." Focusing your attention on where you want to get to, rather than on your mistakes will help. When I'm working with parents who are struggling to get their child's name and pronouns right, I offer a variety of different strategies to practice. You're essentially needing to reprogram your brain, as names and pronouns often come from the unconscious mind, rather than the conscious, particularly if you're stressed or excited.

The key is practice. Below are some examples of strategies I teach and encourage to reprogram your brain.

- Practice saying their name and pronoun out loud, 20

times a day.

- Use their correct name and pronoun, even if they're not around (as long as they're out to the person you're talking to).

- Put their new name on their bedroom door.

- Use the Buddy System – recruit a buddy and have regular conversations using your child's name and pronoun. Kindly point out mistakes and acknowledge and congratulate each other when you get it right.

- Acknowledge and reward your wins.

- Be kind around mistakes – you can say to yourself "I need to practice more".

Communication breakdown and what to do about it

Parents are also often feeling frustrated and even cranky with their kids. Feeling like their kids are not being fair, are impatient, and not understanding how tough it is for them. I totally understand where those feelings are coming from. They feel like they're walking on eggshells, getting in trouble for every little mistake and getting no leniency or understanding, let alone recognition for the effort they're putting in or the times when they do get it right. I get it. It's tough to live in this environment, as we've discussed earlier.

Like anything, there are two sides to every story and because I've been in the privileged position of hearing both sides, I'd like to share the magic elixir to this situation.

In the above situation, communication is breaking down. Everyone is in defensive mode and feels like the other party is not considering their needs. Remember what we spoke about earlier in relation to active, non-defensive listening? Your child needs to feel seen, heard and understood, so they no longer feel the need to fight for it. And of course, so do you. As the parent we could argue that it's your responsibility to lead the way in this situation. How do you do that?

First, I encourage you, again, to make sure you have your own support system in place as it may take some time for your child to shift in their responses. Then it is time to implement the lessons around active, non-defensive listening.

Listen to what your child is telling you, and be vulnerable and willing to learn. If you've already had the conversation, there's no need to rehash it, but you can spend some time reflecting on what they shared and ask for clarity if you need it, they're the experts. Take some time to consider what you need to help you reduce and, in time, eliminate the mistakes. It might be a good time to have that discussion with your child or anyone else that might be helpful. Keep reading and that will become clearer.

Acknowledge to your child that your mistakes are frustrating or upsetting (use their words) for them and from now, you'll make a concerted effort to reduce the number of mistakes you make. Share your needs with them and how they can help you. This part will feel more possible after you've been able to practice active, non-defensive listening with them and had some self-reflection time.

Before you approach this conversation, I have some things for you to consider that have been helpful for other parents and teachers trying to minimise mistakes. Begin with stopping the excuses, justifications, and reasons it's hard and it keeps happening. It's a natural human response to continue to make mistakes or not follow through with change, while ever we continue to make excuses or justify our behaviour. For example, have you ever tried to give up eating chocolate or sugar? Our brain is the best at finding reasons, excuses, or justifications for why we can just have this one little bit, just one time and then we'll stop. "Oh, I'm just going to finish this block of chocolate because once it's gone from the house, I won't want it anymore." Or, "I've had a really tough day, I just need a little pick me up." Or "It's from the organic place, so it won't be that bad for me." Whilst those excuses are there, we have zero chance of quitting chocolate.

The same goes for quitting the old name and pronouns. How do we give up chocolate successfully? We make a rock-solid commitment to ourselves that from now on, no matter what, we're not having any more chocolate. We might also replace it with a healthier snack. You need to do the same for your child's name and pronouns. Make a heartfelt commitment to yourself and your child, to get their name and pronouns correct, from this moment forward. Your commitment is to stop using the old name and pronouns and replace them with the new ones. It will feel strange at first, but the same as replacing chocolate with nuts or fruit will soon become your new normal, and so will their name and pronouns.

Another important aspect of giving up chocolate is to be kind to ourselves if we slip up. Again, the same goes for your child's name and pronouns. The key is not to make excuses. Simply acknowledge you've slipped up and reinforce the commitment you've made to yourself and your child, to get their name and pronouns right. Beating yourself up, telling yourself off, and giving yourself a hard time, will not stop you from eating chocolate. It also will not force you to get their name right. Equally so, making excuses for the mistake will simply give you 'an out' and send the message to your brain that you're not really serious about it. It is definitely a balance. Be firm, commit and be kind and compassionate in the face of a mistake and then recommit and be firm.

So that's how to manage mistakes within yourself. The next question is often, how do I manage when I make the mistake when talking to my child, or within earshot of them? It's similar. Don't make a fuss. Acknowledge your mistake, apologise, and move on. Especially don't make excuses or try to justify your mistake. Avoid trying to convince your child why it's so hard for you. That will have the same impact, on your mind, as we discussed earlier and perhaps more importantly, it sends an unhelpful message to your child. Remember, practice makes perfect.

It may also be worthwhile, to have a follow-up conversation with your child to reiterate that you are sorry and your commitment to getting it right. Be mindful, however, that you're not looking for your child to 'let you off the hook'. It's not their responsibility to make you feel better for your mistake. This is a common mistake that we all make. We over apologise or make a fuss, leaving the trans individual feeling responsible for making you feel better.

In short, acknowledge, apologise, and move on. Avoid excuses, be kind to yourself and recommit to doing better next time. Oh, and avoid expectations on how they should respond. Your mistake might be the 50th mistake they've encountered in their day, even though it might be the first you've made this week.

Struggling with fear or the pressure of having to – 'get it right', all the time, is tough, however as we've discussed above, it's definitely possible, and you are well on your way.

It's important to acknowledge that simply 'getting it right' is not the magic ingredient to repairing the relationship. It's more about deepening your understanding of your child's experience and your emotions, thoughts, and beliefs around it. Once you develop that deeper understanding, you will automatically get it right more often. This doesn't mean you can just put your feet up and leave the rest to chance, but you'll definitely be heading in the right direction.

Repairing your relationship with your child will take time, but it is possible. Communication, understanding, compassion and patience is the key. Doing the work that's been outlined in this book so far is a wonderful place to start, to enable you to approach your child and the situation with a deeper understanding and more compassion for them, yourself, and the circumstances.

MOP ~ Trust your heart and your body

Breathe

Begin with either closing your eyes or softening your gaze out in front. (I know you can't read with your eyes closed, so you'll have to read this through first, remember it and put it into action. Feel free to practice a couple of times first)

TIP – You can record your voice reading these instructions so you can listen to them each time you're going to do this practice. Then there's no need for memory.

With your eyes closed or softened, bring your attention to your body. Do a quick scan of your body. How is it feeling? Do you notice any tension anywhere? Observe without judgement.

Bring your attention to your breath and observe

- No need to alter, judge or analyse. Where do you notice it most? Is it your nostrils, on the inhale or the exhale? Is it your throat, your chest, or your belly?

- Gradually deepen the breath

- In through the nose, out through the nose, if you can. (Use your mouth if needed.) Allow your breath to expand your lungs and your ribcage.

- Deepen further

- Imagine your breath coming all the way to your belly.

- Feel your belly rise as you inhale and lower as you exhale.

- Continue for five breaths (more if you'd like)

- Keep your attention on your breath.

- Your inhale is a guide to connect with yourself.

- Allow your exhale to guide your body to release any tension it may be holding.

- Return

- Allow your breath to return to its natural state.

- When you're ready, open your eyes.

- Do another quick scan of the body. What do you notice? Is there any change?

If it feels helpful, write what you notice in your journal.

After less than 2 minutes, your nervous system has calmed, and your body has relaxed, at least a little.

This now allows you to be much more able to take in what you're about to read. Our mind's capabilities to absorb new information increase significantly when we're calm, our nervous system isn't working overtime, and we're not anxious. For this reason, I'd encourage you to make this a part of your regular practice.

Take Action ~ You've got this!

Space for repair

If you took a break after the MOP, before doing this activity, take a few moments to connect to your breath. Perhaps run through this chapter's MOP one more time. It will be helpful to approach this activity with a calmer nervous system. Have your notebook/journal and pen handy.

Can you remember the moment your child came out?

Where were you? What were you doing?

Imagine you are back at that moment. Reflect on how you felt...

How you responded and/or reacted...

What came up for you at that moment?

Do this with kindness and compassion towards yourself and don't rush it. This is not an opportunity to give yourself a hard time. We're simply reflecting on what actually happened and tapping into the feelings that were present at that moment.

Place both your hands on your heart. Left hand first and right hand on top of the left.

Notice the feelings that were there. They may come up again now.

In a soft gentle voice (either in your head or out loud) share some kind, reassuring words with yourself. Something like: "I did the best I could, with what I had in that moment". "Now is my opportunity to make amends. To apologise to my child."

Remember Maya Angelou's quote I shared in Chapter 3.

"Do the best you can until you know better. Then when you know better, do better."

Now is the time you can do better.

After you've allowed yourself some space, love, and kind, encouraging words, can you take a moment to consider what you'd like to say to your child?

You might find it helpful to write some things down.

I find it helpful to start with what you're hoping the outcome will be. You can use that to check back at the end of this process and ask yourself how likely you think that might be.

For example, when we're stuck in trying to prove ourselves right or defend our actions, the outcome is unlikely to be a resolution of the current problems in a particular situation.

Next write down what feels most important to you, to share with your child. What do you want them to know? How do you want them to feel? How do you want to feel?

Once you have your list, ask yourself, "And what else?" Add anything else that comes up.

Read over your notes and check in with your desired outcome. Do they feel aligned?

Notice how you feel when you're reading what you've written.

There are several options at this point. You can use what you've written to:

- Gain clarity about your feelings and what you'd like to say to them and how (without writing a letter).

- Guide you in writing a letter to your child to give to your child.

- Write the letter and read it to them.

- Write the letter and use it to gain clarity and inform your conversation.

Note: Wait 24 hours before you read your letter or share it with your child. Your brain will process for a while after you complete this exercise. You may then decide to make some alterations to improve your letter and gain more clarity.

Key points

- Take responsibility, show self-compassion, and make it right.

- There is hope for repairing your relationship with your child.

- They're not intentionally trying to get under your skin or make your life harder.

- Active, non-defensive listening is a powerful tool for improving communication.

- The words we use can have a profound effect.

- Make a conscious effort to use new names and pronouns, and with time and repetition, it will become effortless.

Chapter 9

Getting Comfortable

The future is bright

"I wish for days that you wake up and the weight of the world feels light. Days when laughter makes your belly hurt and kind people touch your soul."

~ Mona Lee

You're almost there. That's right, you're at the last chapter, and because you've made it this far, I know you are dedicated to deepening the connection with your child and having the best possible relationship with them. This chapter is all about getting comfortable with them, who they are, how they are in the world and engaging in their lives in the best way you can.

Before we go any further in case the term *comfort level* is making you nervous, I want to assure you, it is a broad term that will look different for everyone at any point in time. They will vary for many reasons, however, what's important for you to understand is that nothing is permanent, including how you feel right now. Your comfort will shift over time, as you do the work and have different experiences. It is a process, so focus your attention there, rather than the destination. My hope for you is that you'll arrive at a place where you can embrace and celebrate your child for who they are, knowing it's a journey and it takes time and effort. Remember to celebrate the wins and beware not to get complacent after reaching a milestone or overcoming a big hurdle, acknowledge your own growth and continue your journey.

In this chapter, we'll explore why it's important to get comfortable, what affects your comfort levels, what happens once you're comfortable and how to show your child that you're comfortable.

Many parents I meet are in the 'I'm ok with it' phase, and while it's an important step along the way, it is also not conducive to the deep, loving, connected relationship you want to have with your child. Would you agree? Let's work together to access and/or deepen your comfortability.

What do I mean by getting comfortable? As I mentioned above, I'm not referring to simply being 'okay' with your child's sexuality and gender. I mean truly comfortable so you can embrace and celebrate them, for exactly who they are. The aim is to become confident talking about sexuality and gender identity, and things like safe sex, affirmative consent, and healthy respectful relationships, as well as a variety of other topics related to LGBTQ+ people. It also includes feeling happy seeing your child with a new partner, witnessing them holding hands, hugging and kissing (not necessarily the 'get a room' type of kissing). Feeling your heart smile when you witness your child in a healthy happy relationship, when they're able to move around in the world relaxed and confident in their own skin. When you can feel the joy with them when they try on new clothes that reflect their gender more accurately, get a new haircut, or receive their name change documentation in the mail. Some of these things might feel confronting at this moment, however, this is the work towards increasing comfort levels.

A helpful guide is if you're comfortable with a similar thing with your straight, cis kids (or other people) then the aim would be to get comfortable with your LGBTQ+ child. If you're not comfortable with some of the above with your straight, cis kids, that's another conversation for us to have, which this process may also assist you in.

Gender is so expansive and the best way you can support your child is to support them with what they're telling you, even if you don't understand. Similar can be said for sexual orientation. The way individuals experience and identify their sexual orientation and gender identity may feel confusing and different or more complex than what you first thought. You don't have to understand but you can acknowledge and reflect back to them what they said to you, how they expressed them- selves and respect that to be their truth.

One quick note before we go any further, please beware of comparing yourself with other parents, it's dangerous. Your journey will be different to others for a variety of reasons and comparing yourself to others, in any circumstances, sets you up for self-judgement and criticism, neither of which are useful. It can, however, be helpful to be curious about other people's journeys, learn from them, take comfort in their stories and connect with others who've had similar experiences. I encourage you to do this when it feels safe to do so.

Now, let's explore how to get comfortable and break down some of those barriers.

The pressure to get it right – let this go

The first step in getting comfortable is to stop punishing yourself and let go of unreasonable expectations so that you can meet yourself with love and kindness. Now of course, I'm not suggesting you meet yourself and bunker down in that spot for the next 6 months, rather take yourself by the hand (I'd be honoured to take your other hand) and take one step at a time, as we've discussed throughout this book.

You'll be surprised, as soon as you let go of the expectation to 'get it right', you'll likely 'get it right' more often. Again, this is not permission to ignore your child's wants and needs in relation to sexuality and gender identity. Remember we talked about a commitment to change and taking personal responsibility to put our learning techniques into practice without punishment and judgement.

The problem with this pressure to get it right is that your self-talk will be encouraging the exact opposite. You'll be saying things, to yourself, like, "I just can't do this", "I can't remember, I'm so used to saying… "(insert old pronouns), "I'm too old for this", "Things have changed so much since I was their age, I have no idea", "I'm such a bad parent, I just can't get it right"… Does any of that sound familiar? All this does is cause unnecessary stress, makes it harder to get it right, reinforces the mistakes and make you feel worse about yourself, your child and/or the situation. We have malleable brains and regardless of our age and history when we focus on wins, take responsibility, persevere, and practice, all those doubts can dissipate.

Understand that you'll make mistakes, we all do, and you will now forgive yourself and reinforce your commitment to yourself and your child to do better next time. Making mistakes is part of learning and teaching us how to do better next time.

Walking on eggshells

Yes, walking on eggshells is exhausting. It is not a way for anyone to live, including you. Why do you feel like you're walking on eggshells? This is often a result of the child's expectations being higher than what the parent is able to meet at a particular point in time. Because your child is in pain and/or struggling they might react in a way that has become difficult to be around.

If you've taken the actions in this book, I feel like it's safe to assume that you're understanding and therefore responses and reactions have improved. What can often happen is that your child does not consciously realise this and therefore continues to react, as a self protective response. Now is a good time for you to reflect on this. Have you taken the steps? Do you honestly feel like you've made significant improvements? If you're still struggling, reach out for some professional support from someone who's not only experienced with LGBTQ+ needs but also those of a parent's journey. That could be me or another suitable professional. You might also like to go back over some sections of this book.

If you do feel like you're responding in more positive ways, but your child is still reacting to you negatively, perhaps it's time for a conversation. Pain doesn't give permission for poor behaviour, there's no need for you to still feel like you're walking on eggshells. However, this conversation will be sensitive. The most helpful response is support and understanding, not punishment. If your child is still young or a teenager, you need to continue to parent they need you to be the adult. They still need boundaries, but they also need support, understanding and guidance on how to manage these big feelings and a space to feel safe to express and explore them. As we talked about earlier, it may feel like a role reversal, but in the big picture, it's not. Yes, they're the expert in how they're feeling, but they may need your help to understand and unpack those feelings. You'll notice when they no longer feel like they need to prove themselves, when they feel seen, heard, and understood, their behaviour will also soften. It may take an open, honest, compassionate conversation(s) for them to let their guard down enough to notice things are changing with you too. They will need some time, love, support and perhaps guidance to heal.

It's also important to note that your child may be experiencing ridicule, abuse or being isolated from other areas in their lives. It's common, particularly if they're a child or adolescent, and safer to take it out on their parents because they know you love them. It's easier to deal with your child's ire if you know you are a safer boxing bag. It's kind of a compliment, albeit unpleasant.

Fake it till you make it – with caution (see section below)

A lot of people suggest to 'fake it till you make it', however, while I feel like that can be helpful, I also feel like it is important to proceed with caution. Yes, in the short term, if you're struggling with your child's sexuality or gender identity, you don't need to tell them. You can choose to do your best to pretend you're okay and get support asap.

There are also situations where you may have an idea of where you'd like to be and intend to work towards that. In these circumstances, faking it can be helpful. It can prevent hurt or damage to your relationship with your child and create space for you to learn, practice and adjust your thinking and/or behaviour. In these circumstances, I would say that 'faking it', is more about holding back your exact feelings, being mindful and tactful in your conversations and responses, not outright lying about how you're feeling.

Let's look at a couple of examples of how this might look in some families I've worked with in the past.

Remember Sally and Jay from chapter 4? Jay let Sally know that they were trans and Sally was convinced that Jay was just a tomboy, like Sally was when she was a child. Sally also deeply valued her relationship with Jay and was terrified she would lose them. She had always prided herself on being a loving, supportive parent, being available to Jay to talk about anything. Jay's gender identity announcement threw her off her parenting values for a little while as she was scared Jay was making a mistake. She was convinced it wouldn't last and was doing her best to protect Jay.

In the context of 'fake it till you make it', what do you think Sally could've done differently?

After working together for a short time, I know Sally certainly had her regrets and wished she'd done things differently. What did she wish, I hear you ask?

She wished she kept her doubts, thoughts, and concerns to herself until she had more time to learn about gender diversity, Jay's feelings and experiences, and the most helpful approaches to take, as well as process her own feelings. She now realises, after a lot of support, learning and encouragement, that it's not helpful to her or Jay, to beat herself up, however, she is able to recognise that it would've been more helpful for them both to keep those things to herself, initially. It would've bought her and Jay some time.

What difference would it have made? It would've allowed Jay the space to explore their gender without having to fight Sally and focus mostly on proving themselves to her. This would've given Jay the opportunity to get clear on how they were feeling and the steps they wanted to take, sooner and with less struggle. It would've meant a lot less conflict in the home and less stress for Sally.

When we talk about faking it, we're not suggesting that you should ignore your feelings, rather, avoid sharing them with your child, until you've had the time and space to process, learn and understand more about your child's experience and what you're feeling.

B.S. radar – they'll see straight through you

You also need to know that LGBTQ+ folk have a powerful B.S. radar. They'll see straight through you if you BS them. I know, I know... How can I suggest you 'fake it till you make it' and in the very next paragraph tell you that their BS radar will see straight through you? You're right, it's confusing and contradictory, but bear with me for a minute and I'll explain.

If you try to pretend, you're feeling the complete opposite of what you are, they will pick up on it. If you try to convince them that you're not struggling at all, they will not believe you. There is a difference between omitting the detail and totally contradicting the reality.

Sally, for example, wished she had kept her doubts, thoughts, and concerns to herself. On the flip side, Jay's BS radar would've been on high alert if she'd pretended she was 100% okay with everything. If she'd immediately supported any changes Jay wanted to make and booked them a doctor's appointment to begin the medical process, Jay would've known something was off.

When humans sense something is off, that there's information missing or notice a gap in someone's communication with them, the automatic response is to fill that gap with their own information. It's what we do. We're experts at it. Have you ever been in a situation where one of your loved ones appears to be upset or angry, but they don't want to talk about it and then your brain goes haywire, scanning the last 24 hours to ascertain where you went wrong? Questioning what you did to upset them? Why they're mad at you? You ask them, "Are you mad at me?" They reply, "No, it's not you." You're convinced it must be. Your mind is going a million miles an hour trying to figure it out, only to find out later that day, what's actually wrong with them and it wasn't you.

Does this sound familiar? Can you recall a similar situation in your life? The reason you're convinced you did something wrong is because, like the rest of the human race, your brain needs answers, you're filling the gaps. We commonly assume that because they won't tell us it must be us that did something wrong or caused the situation. Or if we can read that they're holding something back, we scan for what it might be. Now of course depending on the situation we do not always jump to self-blame, however, we do fill the gap with whatever story we are more inclined to fill it with, depending on our default internal responses and other circumstances.

In this alternative scenario, we created for Sally and Jay, Jay would likely fill the gaps created by recognising that Sally wasn't being honest, with thoughts like, "Mum doesn't support me, love me and/or believe me". As you can see, the result is the complete opposite of what Sally intended. Sally would've been overcompensating because she wanted Jay to think she was 'cool' with it, when, in reality, she was in complete internal turmoil. Jay seeing straight through her, though not knowing the truth, created a much worse scenario in their own mind, to fill in the gaps.

Instead, Sally could've let Jay know that she'd always love them and be there for them and that whilst she didn't completely understand what Jay was telling her, she would do her best to learn. She could've let Jay know that she needed a little time to process this news and to learn more, however, nothing would ever stop her from loving them. Then she could ask Jay for a bit of time to do the research and process the news, as well as reassure Jay that they could come to her if they needed support.

An extra tip for Sally and anyone else in this situation:

Because the time it'll take Sally to do her research and processes her thoughts and feelings will feel like forever to Jay, it's important that Sally is clear about what Jay can expect next. For example, Sally could ask Jay, "Would it be ok if we check in next week? What about we go for pizza on Friday night and check in with each other?" This reassures Jay that Sally is still there for them, she wants to better understand, and she's not trying to sweep it under the rug. It also makes it easier for them both to bring the conversation up again, because there's been an expectation set. Keeping in mind, it would not be advised for Sally to make any promises she doesn't know she can keep. For example, suggesting they have pizza on Friday night to talk about things, because she will have had enough time to learn and process what she's feeling.

Having worked with hundreds of young people and parents, and having the privilege of hearing both sides, a common communication breakdown point is exactly this. *Returning to the conversation after the initial 'coming out'.* Both parties make assumptions about the other, they struggle to know how to bring it up again, "Should I bring it up again? When should I bring it up?" When this happens the good old, human gap filler, goes to work. Parents assume that their kids don't want to talk about it, or that they're ok and there's nothing to say, or they're mad at me and avoiding it, or something similar. The child (of any age) thinks the parents don't want to talk about it, "they've swept it under the carpet and want to pretend it didn't happen. They're against it so want to ignore it. They're freaking out, so won't talk to me." Either way, both could benefit from talking about it, even for just a few minutes to touch base and clear up any assumptions and gain a better understanding of how everyone's feeling.

The key is to find the sweet spot. I know, easier said than done, but definitely possible. Remember to be authentic, and if you're struggling, only share what's necessary. Keep it short and sweet and schedule a follow-up conversation. You've got this!!!

The power of internal conversations

The power of internal conversations is incredible. It is a power that many of us overlook. Becoming aware of your self-talk and its impact can make an enormous difference to how you feel, in any circumstance. When it comes to your child's sexuality or gender identity, it's no different. What you tell yourself will impact how you feel.

One of the strategies I use with the people I work with, not just parents, is to increase their awareness of their thoughts and their level of helpfulness. Becoming aware of your internal conversations provides you with an opportunity to reflect on whether they're helpful and adapt accordingly. Changing thought patterns is not the easiest task to embark on by yourself, but it is possible.

I use a therapeutic approach called ACT (Acceptance and Commitment Therapy, created by Steven C. Hayes). In ACT we're not interested in whether a thought is true or false, but rather whether it's helpful. That might sound a bit strange but think of it this way; a mother is ruminating over the unkind words that were said to her child. Whether or not those words were spoken (true or false) is not an important element at this point. It's whether it is helpful, or not, to keep playing it over and over in her mind. In this case, it may be true that the words were said, and that her child is hurt and upset, however ruminating on it isn't helping her or her child. It's upsetting her and interfering with her ability to be present for her child. It inhibits her ability to meet the child's needs and/or being able to effectively address the situation with the person who made the unkind comments. This sort of thinking has the potential to paralyse her with anger and fear of confrontation.

If the thought is helpful, great, you can go with it. If it's unhelpful, like the above example, some might suggest you need to change them or get rid of them. Have you ever tried to do that? What happened? Are you like many others and find that the thought you're trying to change or push away seems to persist and often get bigger and stronger than ever? This strategy can be helpful for some people in some circumstances, however for many it results in a battle of thoughts. As they're trying to push them away, change them or suppress them it becomes a battle inside them.

Please note: Most experts would suggest we seek professional support to gain the best outcomes when practising therapeutic techniques. Reading instructions gives us an intellectual understanding which can be helpful, however, it doesn't always translate into effective practice. Reading can help you get started in the process. It can inspire you to seek support to deepen your learning. Professional support will often increase motivation and makes the process easier, more effective, and ensures we understand the nuances.

When we're in battle, or fighting something, it means that we are focused on that thing. Have you heard the saying, 'What you focus on, you get more of'? That's what happens with your thoughts. If you're fighting them, you're focussing on them, and they can then become more powerful. In ACT, we're encouraged to simply acknowledge them and detach from them. They call it cognitive diffusion. Keep in mind, stress causes negative or unhelpful thoughts to be more powerful, therefore it is strongly suggested to seek help with this process. This kind of approach is much more effective when practised under the guidance of a therapist or counsellor. There are a few different ways of doing this. It all begins with becoming more aware of your thoughts and noticing which ones are helpful and which ones are not. If you'd like to explore this further, you know where I am.

As we've discussed earlier, a common concern for parents is that their child will be bullied or mistreated in some way. This often results in parents playing a variety of scenarios over and over in their minds, causing an enormous amount of stress a worry. As I'm writing this, the parents of a 13-year-old, I worked with a few years ago, come to mind. They were both worried about their child being bullied at school, so they told their child not to come out at school. This had several implications for their child, the parents, and their family.

They reached out to me after they'd realised that this approach wasn't working. Here's what they shared:

- Their child had withdrawn from their friends, school-work, and after-school activities.

- The parents were fighting a lot, because of differing opinions on how to manage the situation and feeling overwhelmed with the worry.

- Their child had stopped communicating with them and was spending most of their time in their bedroom

- Their child's grades had dropped, and so had their appetite.

The parents were beside themselves with worry for their child and had no idea which way to turn.

After a brief conversation with their child, I was able to ascertain that while their parents were doing their best to try to protect them, what had actually occurred, was that they had implied to their child that there was something wrong with them and that it should be kept a secret. The burden of the secret, the shame and the fear had become too much for their child to manage. It was easier for them to withdraw than to take the risk of others finding out the truth. It was easier than pretending to be someone that they weren't. They also felt like they didn't deserve their friends and their sense of self-worth had plummeted.

Unfortunately, this is a common occurrence. In pursuit of protecting our kids, we often end up inadvertently causing harm. Thankfully these parents recognised the problem quite quickly and the repair process was fast. What they discovered was they had projected their fear onto their child. Their fear and worry had almost paralysed them. They were unable to see any other way through this situation. They were unable to communicate with each other in an effective way, as they were both so weighed down by their own fears, worry, and guilt.

After just one (two hour) session they were able to recognise the power their unhelpful thoughts were having over them. They began the process of cognitive diffusion and felt the weight lifting almost immediately. Of course, this was a process and everything didn't change, overnight. However, they did notice a shift quite soon. They began by having an open discussion with their child, acknowledging they had made a mistake by prohibiting them from sharing the truth about themselves. They acknowledged that it wasn't their life to make decisions over and though they were trying to protect their child, they could now see this was a mistake. They shared with their child that they were seeing someone that was helping them to do a better job and asked if they would mind waiting a couple of weeks to give them a bit of time to learn how to best support them, so as to not make similar mistakes in the future.

There was a huge weight lifted off all of them. Their child was happy to wait (with a fixed timeframe named) and relieved to have the breathing space themselves. The parents' communication improved, over time, as they both realised, they had the same goals. Suddenly, their child returned to the shared family spaces, they were sharing meals together again and able to have open conversations.

Of course, this family had a bit of a journey ahead of them, however, they had taken the first steps and the relief they felt from those was very welcome. It gave them all hope for their future. This shift came about because the parents, with support and guidance, started to recognise how unhelpful their thoughts were and began to name them the 'fear story'.

Did their fear disappear? No! Did their worry disappear? No! What changed was that there was much less ruminating and they stopped making their decisions through fear. Using ACT they learned to recognise, acknowledge, and name their unhelpful thoughts as their 'fear story', which took the power out of the story and gave them the space to breathe and think about some alternatives. Instead of requiring their child hides their identity, they became informed and equipped with strategies to best support them. They learned how the school managed sexual and gender diversity, what they had in place to protect students and what their policies and procedures were. The parents eventually became advocates for their child in their school, their sporting club and all other environments their child wished to spend time in.

This is one example of parents beginning to shift out of fear, into a more comfortable space and how that can impact everyone in the family. Please understand that this was a process for the family. It didn't happen overnight, however, some lightness did come very quickly. It wasn't easy. They had to work at it. They made a commitment to their child, themselves, each other, and their family unit. They took small actions often and life became easier each time, as a result.

Please note, while these parents were able to recognise the power of those unhelpful thoughts, this is not always the case. Please do not compare yourself to this family, or expect the same for yourself. It can take one, a few or many sessions and in this case, we were talking about specific thoughts. Like most things, the more you practice, the more embedded it becomes. People need more than one session to work through and unpack what's going on for them.

Your role, your influence

This leads us to explore your role in your child's life, and the influence you have on them and anyone around them. Don't underestimate the power you have to create change in your life and in your child's life. We began to demonstrate this in the last section, but it doesn't stop there.

Ease your way in. In the beginning, no one expects you to start marching the streets with giant placards. Remember every little step has an impact, and you may never attend a march, but you'll show your support in other ways. We'll explore how to be an effective ally a little later in this chapter, however, I want you to understand how important your role is in your child's life. It always has been, and now is no different. In fact, it is even more crucial.

Your child will likely be hyperalert to your comments, behaviours, facial expressions, and body language. I'm not telling you this to make you nervous or self-conscious, rather to highlight how important it is for you to get comfortable, to be authentic and to find a way you can feel relaxed around your child and have conversations with and about them. Not only will you be sending a loving, supportive message to them, you'll also be a role model to others, in how to treat your child and other LGBTQ+ folk.

Jason

Remember Jason, from chapter 3? He was worried about how his colleagues would react if he came out about his LGBTQ+ child. The culture of his workplace didn't feel inclusive at all. There were often jokes made and unpleasant comments in response to the representation of LGBTQ+ people in the media and no one seemed to challenge these. Jason decided not to share the news about his child right away and instead embarked on a mission to create change within his workplace.

Over his next couple of sessions, we brainstormed and crafted a variety of ways that Jason could become a gentle, but effective role model on how to be respectful, inclusive and supportive of the LGBTQ+ community, without risking 'outing' his child and himself before he was ready. He went about planting small seeds, encouraging more inclusive conversations and behaviours. As he did, to his surprise, a couple of his colleagues approached him to thank him because they were also uncomfortable with the culture around sexuality and gender identity. One of those conversations even prompted the suggestion that the workplace undergo some Equity, Diversity, and Inclusion (EDI) training.

Eventually, Jason decided with his child's consent that it was time to be more open in his workplace. He planned to use the EDI training as an opportunity to share that he had his own personal experience. He felt like it would give the training more context, purpose, and impact if the staff knew someone that it directly affected. He admitted it felt like there was safety in numbers, so doing it in the training would mean that there were also more allies in the room. He didn't plan to 'out' his child at that point. He just wanted to share that this topic impacted him personally, and the encouraging response he received, prompted him to share more.

Jason was able to do this because he had done the work to build his level of comfortability and confidence about his child's identity. It wasn't always like that for Jason. When I first met him, he really struggled. He'd come so far. Both his ability to share the truth in a clear and confident manner and the groundwork he'd been doing earlier by role-modelling appropriate behaviour had placed him in a position of respect. He influenced his whole workplace. That's 80 more individuals in the world who are better educated and informed, have real-life examples of how to behave and have increased awareness, understanding and compassion. Arguably, the world is a better place because of Jason's courage and commitment to learn and share.

Be vulnerable to life's lessons – you'll learn quicker

This is a powerful quote I heard a while ago and felt like it was meant to be shared with you. All the work that's being asked of you right now is ultimately asking you to be vulnerable, open and courageous. For some of you, this will be a long way from your comfort zone and that's ok. Go at your own pace, get the support you need, and keep in mind that when you continue to move forward, regardless of how small your steps are, you'll eventually get to where you want to be.

Step out of your comfort zone, be prepared to learn new things, hear other perspectives, and adapt your thinking to enable a deeper understanding and in turn, connection with your child. And throughout the process, remember the key words – 'kindness and compassion' to yourself, effective learning doesn't occur through punishment, judgement, criticism, and fear.

Create a safe space for your child to explore their identity and be themselves

Do you remember when you were a child and you 'just knew' some things were not talked about? This happens because of overt discussions and behaviour and through more subtle messaging, including the omission of specific topics. A common mistake I hear from parents is their assumption that their child knows that it's okay to talk about certain things or that it's safe and okay in their family to be different. This occurs before and after their child comes out. The parents I've worked with and talked to about this have often shared that they are "leaving it up to them to bring up the subject when they're ready to talk about it. I don't want to pressure them or make everything about their sexuality/gender identity."

The problem with that is, their child often feels like their parent doesn't want to talk about it, or that it's not okay. They may also think that everyone wants to pretend it's not true, that it's gone away. It's like they 'came out' and then got shoved straight back in, which can feel so difficult because the coming out conversation took so much courage and now they don't know how to bring it up again.

Your child has taken a mammoth leap of faith by sharing with you in the first place. It's now your role to keep the conversation open and on the table. It's true, your child is many things other than their sexuality or gender identity and they likely don't want the focus to always be on that. However, it's also important that you create opportunities for discussion and check-ins, so they know you haven't swept it under the carpet.

Another mistake parents often make (when their child is not an adult when they first come out) is to put new rules in place that they intend to protect their child but can in fact cause more harm. An example of that is banning their child from having sleepovers with friends of the same sex, after coming out as gay. Or insisting the bedroom door is left open when a friend is visiting. This rarely works out well. I'll share an experience of a family I worked with a couple of years ago after their 15-year-old child came out as gay, and how we worked through it to repair the relationship and deepen the connection within the family.

Cynthia, Geoff and Thomas

Cynthia and Geoff responded to their son coming out as gay reasonably well. They had close family friends who were gay and had suspected their son Thomas was also gay for many years. In a way, they were preparing themselves for that moment for some time and had even asked their friends for some guidance. Everything went fairly smoothly at first, and the family shared that they were all a bit relieved that it was out in the open.

The problems began when Thomas's male friend came over for a visit and then asked if he could sleep over. This was the first visit since Thomas came out. They had been friends for several years and sleepovers were a common occurrence. The difference this time was the parents said no, with no apparent reason. After a small amount of squabbling, Thomas accepted their response, for the moment, anyway. However, once the friend left and the parents approached Thomas with the new household rules, he was furious, frustrated and upset.

The new rules were that there were to be no more sleepovers with male friends unless they were happy to sleep in the spare room and the bedroom door was to now stay open, at all times, when friends were visiting. To make things worse, his female friends were still not allowed to sleep over, and the bedroom door had to remain open when they visited too. You can just imagine how all this went down. Yep! Like a lead balloon!

Thomas was 15 years old, his friends were always welcome to visit and stay, in the past. There were rules, but not like these. He felt like he was being punished for being gay.

We've all heard these rules before, even if they didn't exist in your home. It's common practice in many families, including family shows on TV and movies. It's no surprise to hear that boys and girls are not allowed to have sleepovers, or that the bedroom doors must remain open when they're visiting. So it makes sense that once your child shares that they're attracted to people of the same sex, these rules would be adjusted, right? On the surface, it sounds reasonable. I agree. However, if we look a little deeper into what messages are bound up in there, as well as what opportunities are missed, regardless of the gender of the friends and your child's sexuality, it is huge.

Needless to say, these new rules created huge conflict in the house. They isolated Thomas from his friends and sent a message of distrust to their child. The new rules also made Thomas think that his parents don't 'get it' and perpetuated the myth that gay people are attracted to everybody of the same gender. It resulted in a shutting down of communication and created a tense, uncomfortable, hostile family environment. Thomas shut down completely. He spent all his time in his room, wouldn't share a meal with the family and withdrew from friends because it was embarrassing to have to tell them why his parents had implemented these new rules.

The other piece the parents are missing here is that Thomas has always been gay. Every time he had sleepovers in the past, every time his friends visited, the door was closed. The only difference is that they now have more information about their son, he trusted them to invite them into his world and it felt to him like they had responded by saying you can't be trusted with your friends anymore.

I get it! We all want to keep our kids safe. We don't want them having sex or finding themselves in intimate situations before they're ready. Or is it before we're ready? The thing is, banning sleepovers or enforcing bedroom doors to be open does not prevent these things from happening, regardless of the sexuality or gender of your child and their friends. It might make it a little more difficult, but the reality is, if they want it to happen, it will. Unfortunately, it'll mean that it's more likely to be in an unsafe situation, with less accurate information and with less ability to navigate the situation in a healthy respectful way. They're also less likely to be able to turn to you for support or advice if they need it.

I'm not suggesting you can't have your family values, beliefs and rules, however, take some time to reflect on their purpose and whether they are actually effective in achieving the outcomes you're looking for. From my experience, as a parent and from working with hundreds of young people and their families, oh and yes, I was a teenager once, too, it's much more helpful and likely to ensure your child's safety if you can keep the communication open and trust your child. Perhaps a compromise can be negotiated that suits both.

This is all part of getting comfortable. We need to create spaces where you and your child can have conversations about healthy relationships, sexual health, self-respect, respecting others and consent. If you're concerned about your child becoming intimate with someone under your roof, talk about it, in an adult way, not shaming, guilting or judging your child. There are a bunch of strategies you can use that don't create the tension, conflict and shutting down that these rules created for Thomas and his parents. If you'd like to know more, let's talk, I'd love to work through this with you.

What are some other ways you can create safe spaces for your child to explore their identity? You can offer to go shopping with them, browse the internet with them for haircuts that might suit them, talk about relationships you see depicted in the media, ask them about their interests, and be generally curious about them and their lives. Find any way you can to let them know that anything they want to 'try on' in relation to their identity is okay in your home and in your family. Make sure they know that you celebrate differences and are proud of them for their ability to explore themselves.

Allyship – becoming an effective ally

Allyship is another wonderful way you can let your child know they are safe, loved and supported in your family, exactly how they are.

An ally is a person who'll stand and speak up for others in tough or uncomfortable situations. Saying no to unfair, unjust behaviours, bullying, exclusion, and physical and emotional abuse. It may occur on a micro or macro level. Micro settings include, but are not limited to, a schoolyard, work lunchroom, bus stop, shopping centre or a family home. Macro is referring to organisations and systems, like governments and organisational policies, for example.

Being an effective ally can be overt, like saying something to let others know their behaviour is inappropriate or more subtle, like standing next to somebody and letting them know that they're not alone. It can also be advocating in your child's school, challenging systems within governments or workplaces. Every little bit helps to get us closer to a safer, more inclusive society.

It might take you time before you feel equipped or ready to be an effective ally, but I want you to know that you can make a difference and send a helpful message to your child in a variety of ways. Reading this book and increasing your knowledge and understanding is a huge step in the right direction. Continuing your journey of becoming more comfortable, will enable you to have helpful conversations and not tolerate inappropriate behaviours. Over time you'll become more confident and find ways you can speak up for your child and contribute to the fight for safety, love and inclusion for all.

There are a variety of ways a parent can be a great ally for their child. To find out more, you can check out the 'How to be the Best Ally' guide, in the resources section of my website. In the meantime, I can offer the following suggestions:

- Ensure that your child knows you have their back. To do this you will need to continue the work you're currently doing to educate yourself and become more comfortable.

- Don't ignore or allow inappropriate comments and behaviour from others.

- Be a good role model.

- Advocate for them when they need you to

- Expand others' minds - continue to learn and share what you learn with others.

- Your child won't necessarily expect you to attend Pride Parades and events, though that would be a beautiful indication that you're 100% behind them, but only when you're ready.

Creating change is definitely a numbers game, so make sure your voice is heard. Please remember this is a journey and to become an effective ally is a process. Take one step at a time and do what you can.

Tolerance, acceptance, embracing, celebration

Tolerance, acceptance, embracing, and celebration are all terms that are bantered around when discussing sexuality and gender identity. I'm sure you've heard some or all of them. You may have also heard people say that tolerance and acceptance are not okay. Your child may have even said this to you. Let's explore why.

Celebrating your child for exactly who they are is the epitome of *getting comfortable*. And maybe you're not quite there yet, so what's wrong with tolerance or acceptance? Before I explain, I want to encourage you to approach this section with love and kindness to yourself. There's no room for judgement or criticism here and I hope you've been able to let that go a couple of chapters ago, or at least be working on it.

I'm going to cut straight to it, and if you want to know more you can check out my blog, 'Do you accept your LGBTQ+ child? – Why that's not enough.'

What I want you to remember, is that language is powerful. The words we say can have a significant impact on those around us and different words will impact different people in a variety of ways. I want to assure you that we're not talking about semantics or political correctness, here. We're talking about kindness, compassion, consideration, understanding, love, and support.

"Language shapes the way we think and determines what we can think about".

~ Benjamin Lee Whorf

We're going to focus on four words. As you read them consider which one most closely relates to how you feel about your child. Be honest, growth can't happen if you're lying to yourself.

Tolerate – Accept – Embrace – Celebrate

If you said embrace or celebrate, fantastic, continue on and enjoy yourself. If you didn't, that's okay, because this is our goal and we can work towards, it together. First, you need to understand why tolerance, or even acceptance is not good enough. You may have heard someone else say this and feel like they're being overly sensitive.

Let's consider the feelings and true meaning behind these words when we're talking about human beings, people we love, care about, respect or simply walk by in the street.

You or someone you know may have innocently used expressions such as, "I tolerate..." or "I accept..." While accepting someone is an improvement to tolerating them, there are implications behind these words that you may not be conscious of. Let's take a closer look so you can get a bit more insight into why people react the way they do.

Is it ok to tolerate someone?

Tolerating someone is better than hating them or being outright rude, abusive, or discriminatory towards them, however, it's not considerate, respectful, loving or kind, either. When I think about the word 'tolerate', the words, 'put up with' come to mind. It implies there is something wrong with the person, and you'll give them the 'privilege' of you tolerating them or their behaviour. You don't agree with it or think it's ok, you don't like it, but you'll tolerate it, because you feel like, or have been told that this is the right thing to do.

When I put it like that, it feels quite unpleasant, don't you think? No one wants to be simply tolerated and I certainly don't want to just tolerate people I care about. Sure, we don't have to be besties with everyone. We're not always going to see eye to eye with others. We're all different and we all have different personalities, interests, values, beliefs, weaknesses and strengths. But life is short, and time is precious and simply tolerating people (especially our children), for who they are, doesn't feel like a great use of energy, to me.

I can't tell you how to feel and you may already be past the tolerating stage, my aim is to shine some light on why this term is hurtful, why it's important to work your way along the continuum and/or guide others to do the same.

What about acceptance? It's okay, right?

Hmmm... sure, it's certainly a step up from tolerance. Though, it may feel like it's still suggesting there's something wrong with the person that the rest of us have to, or want to accept. When we say we accept something, we are saying that we'll manage, we'll learn or have learned to live with it, or yes, it's ok (but not great). For example, it could feel like you're saying, "I accept that you're gay", but consciously or subconsciously, "I don't really like it". Or "I accept that you're going to change your university course", but, consciously or subconsciously, I'm not too thrilled about it. Not really bad, but not too great either.

I absolutely understand that if a person is accepting of another person's sexuality or gender identity, their intention is not to be harmful. And to be honest, for many people, they won't feel too badly about it. Often, they'll be relieved and happy to be accepted. Unfortunately, that's because the alternative is to be rejected, or worse. For most LGBTQ+ folk, when they're considering 'coming out' or 'inviting others in', their expectations are quite low. And the anticipation and/or fear is high. In short, acceptance is okay, however, don't you want to do more than just accept your child?

Striving to celebrate and embrace your child.

What about the alternatives? The ones to strive for?

Embracing feels much better, don't you think? It feels more loving, kind and warm. Embracing your LGBTQ+ loved one is sending a very clear message that "I love you, exactly how you are". There are no conditions, ifs, or buts. You're inviting them to be themselves around you and encouraging an open, loving, supportive relationship.

The next stop... Celebration!!!

Now here's a delightful way to feel and talk about our loved ones. "I love and celebrate everything about my child, sibling, parent, aunt, uncle, cousin, grandparent, or friend." It still doesn't mean you have to agree with them on every topic, but they are a whole person, with many different aspects to them, and how delightful to love and celebrate them as a wonderful human being in your life.

I'm not asking you to jump on a float at Mardi Gras or the next Pride event, though feel free to if you feel inspired to because I'm sure you'd have a load of fun.

This is more about your thoughts and feelings and how you speak to and about your child. Challenging the idea that there is something to be tolerated or accepted and instead, embracing and celebrating them as a whole being, for exactly who they are.

Our lives become much richer when we celebrate diversity and see and experience differences as strengths, rather than weaknesses and reasons to judge and criticise.

It's important to remember that language is powerful, the words we choose to use can cause hurt, pain, sadness, rejection and disconnection. The flip side of that is we can also choose words that create a sense of safety, love, warmth, inclusion, and beautiful connections. Choose your language wisely. Do it from the heart, rather than from fear. Use it as an opportunity to keep the light burning inside their heart by reassuring them, they are loved, appreciated, and celebrated, exactly how they are.

Ask questions – be curious and interested

A great place to finish up and what better way to test your comfort level, is to ask questions, and get curious and interested in their lives. Create and participate in conversations with them, as you would if your child was straight and cis. Be interested in their social lives, their relationships, crushes, shopping experiences, fashion, sports, hobbies, music etc. Be mindful of any avoidance or reluctance to discuss topics that may not feel comfortable, yet. They'll only become comfortable with practice, so get started.

Parents often ask me; "Is it okay to ask my child...?" Or "How do I know if it's ok to ask?" There are a couple of golden rules that I'll share with you and aside from that I encourage you to take the risk of becoming that 'awkward' parent who asks too many questions. (don't let your child read that bit, haha)

Do your research!

At the risk of sounding like a broken record; the questions you ask need to be about your child and their lives and not an educational opportunity for you about sexuality and gender identity. Your education is not their responsibility. Do your own research. Even if they appear to not mind, it's not their job to get you up to speed. Unfortunately, it's a burden that LGBTQ+ folk carry in many areas of their lives, don't be part of that. Investing in your own learning also sends a clear message to your child that you care enough to put in the effort.

Is it okay to ask your LGBTQ+ child?

If you're not sure whether it's appropriate to ask, put it to the 'straight, cis child, test'. That is, would you ask your other kids the same question? If the answer is yes, then it's probably okay. You may just need to be a little more gentle or sensitive to their feelings and needs. If the answer's no, ask yourself why you wouldn't ask your straight, cis child, but would want to ask your LGBTQ+ child. In this circumstance it's probably not a good idea, however, there may be some scenarios where it's okay. Before you ask, check in with yourself, do you need to know the answer? Can you get the answer from elsewhere? How do you think your child will feel? How will you and/or them benefit from the question being asked and answered?

Avoid assumptions!

Never make assumptions, they're dangerous. They often don't turn out well. If you're unsure ask, either your child or if it's appropriate, someone else. If it's about your child's personal experience, they are the only ones that can answer accurately, however, sometimes it can be helpful to get a bigger picture of others' experiences first, so you can be more prepared with some insight.

When to ask?

Pick your timing. Don't do those personal awkward questions in front of others. Avoid questions when they appear tired, stressed, upset, or cranky. If it feels like it might be a deeper conversation, allow them some time to 'warm up' to it. Don't spring it on them, out of the blue. Just because you're thinking about it doesn't mean they are. It can often help to ask them if now, is a good time for them to have a chat. Think about past experiences and how they like to be approached. Do they like warnings, do they like to be asked, or are they more spontaneous etc?

After many years of working with young people, I can tell you that potentially challenging, uncomfortable, or awkward conversations are often easier to have in the car or going for a walk. Keeping their privacy in mind, so not with others in the car or crowded spaces where it is likely the conversation will be overheard.

Who to ask?

Sometimes your child won't be the right person to ask, either because they're not ready for answering questions, or like I mentioned earlier, it's not their job to educate you. Where do you get your answers from if you can't ask your child? Of course, you can always ask me, but you already know that, right? Yes, Google can be a wonderful source of information, however, please be careful you're using a reputable source. Social media can also be quite helpful, for other parents, LGBTQ+ people themselves and professionals with experience. Again, be mindful that not everyone is a great resource. Do your homework and trust your gut...only trust your gut after you have done your homework. Don't believe everything everyone says. We are all influenced by our own experiences and another person's experience may not fit yours and your child's experience and circumstances.

This one should be obvious by now, but in case it's not, many people will say that it's not about you. It is about you, too. Understand most of those people are well-intentioned and part of what they say is true. You do need to support your child. That means doing the work so that you can show up for your child in a way that helps them to thrive.

MOP ~ Trust your heart and your body

Hands to your heart

You're almost at the end and you've done incredibly well.

It's time to connect with your heart.

Take a few minutes to connect with your breath. Allow it to gradually deepen.

As you've done in earlier MOPs, allow your exhale to guide your body to release any tension.

Place your hands on your heart. Left hand first, right hand on top of your left.

Notice your hands connected to your skin, your chest. Feel the rise and fall of your chest.

Notice what's just beyond your hands.

(this is not a thinking exercise. I'm not asking you to think about what's there, rather focus on the sensation of your hand connecting to your body, notice what's just beyond your hands. What do you sense?)

Allow yourself at least a few minutes to sit with this feeling, simply noticing.

Notice what you feel...

If it feels helpful, write it in your journal.

Take Action ~ You've got this!

Remember What You Love About Them

Write down all the things you love about your child.

You may need to take a moment to allow your mind to wander back to before you heard this news. Imagine them when you knew they were on their way, as a newborn, a three-year-old, an eight-year-old and when they were eleven. What can you remember about them?

What did you love then?

What are their quirks?

What are their strengths?

What kinds of things do they do that make you laugh or smile?

What do you admire in them?

What have they done that made you proud? What have you bragged about?

What causes that little flutter in your heart?

Use this list to remind yourself that your child is a lot of things, and their sexuality and gender identity are only one part of that picture.

Keep this list handy, as a reminder. Keeping sight of who they are and what you love about them will help reduce the overwhelm because these things haven't changed. They're still the same person. You just have more information about them.

Key Points

- Your child has an exceptional BS radar – they'll see straight through you if your try to pretend you're ok when you're not.

- The pressure to get it right is real, be kind to yourself and commit to your learning.

- Fake till you make it – with caution (remember point one).

- Ask questions – be curious and interested.

- The power of internal conversations – explore the impact – self-reflection.

- Remember you can have a significant influence on their wellbeing and resilience.

- Be vulnerable to life's lessons – it's the best way to grow.

- Create a safe space for your child so they can safely and comfortably explore their identity and be themselves.

- Practice, learn and deepen your understanding so you can become your child's number one ally.

- Work towards embracing and celebrating your child, rather than simply tolerating, and accepting.

Acknowledgments

To my family and friends, thank you for your ongoing encouragement, support and belief in me and my life adventures. To my kids, thank you for your sacrifices while I pursued my dreams to become a social worker and for your deep love, support and encouragement throughout the ups and downs we call life. I feel your love and pride in my heart and am forever grateful.

I'd like to express my deepest gratitude to the following individuals whose unwavering support, guidance, and inspiration have been instrumental in the creation of this book:

Jane, thank you for your exceptional editing skills, in this book and a lifetime of support. Your unwavering belief in me, encouragement, and dedication to my growth have been invaluable. You have shaped the content of this book and inspired me to be the best version of myself—a strong, independent woman. Your impact on my journey cannot be overstated.

Susanne, your editing expertise, and unwavering support have played a crucial role in this book's development and completion. Your encouragement and mentoring to step out of my comfort zone and serve LGBTQI+ young people and their families have been transformative. Your presence in my life has been a constant source of inspiration, and I am truly grateful for your guidance, encouragement, and friendship.

Jen, you've been my rock throughout the development of Indigo Journey and the inception of this book. Your unwavering support, availability as a sounding board, voice of reason, and shoulder to cry on have been immeasurable. I am grateful for your belief in me, my abilities, and my dreams. Your love and support have been an essential and much appreciated part of this journey.

Jami, I am profoundly grateful for the opportunity you offered me to step into my dream job and support LGBTQI+ young people and their families. Your mentorship, encouragement, and unwavering belief in my abilities have been instrumental in my journey. You have consistently been a source of inspiration, motivating me to give my utmost and find the courage to persevere even in the face of adversity.

To my writing buddies, Stacey and Kristy, thank you for your support and contributions. Stacey, your encouraging voice and therapeutic reflections at the beginning of this writing journey were much appreciated. Kristy, your excitement, passion, and expertise infused my writing process with inspiration and motivation. Your presence and guidance have been a tremendous asset.

Casey, I want to extend my deepest appreciation for your generosity and assistance with the book cover. Your valuable insight, guidance, and support were instrumental in shaping the final outcome. Your willingness to lend your expertise and go above and beyond has made a significant impact. Thank you for being an integral part of this creative process.

Lastly, I want to express my deepest gratitude to all the young people, parents, and families who have allowed me the privilege of walking alongside you on your journey. Your trust, courage, hard work, and commitment to the process have been awe-inspiring. This book is both for and because of you, and I am forever grateful for your belief in yourselves and each other.

Thank you all for being integral parts of this journey and for your unwavering support. This book is a testament to the power of collaboration, inspiration, and the collective commitment to creating a better world for LGBTQI+ people, their families, and our communities.

Land Acknowledgments

We respectfully acknowledge the traditional custodians of the lands on which this book was created, edited and published. We pay our deepest respects to the Wadawurrung People (Australia) and the Musqueam, Squamish and Tsleil-Waututh People (Canada), who have been the stewards of these lands for generations.

We recognize that these lands hold deep cultural, historical, and spiritual significance. We honour the enduring connection between the Indigenous communities and their traditional lands, waters, and all living beings. As we engage with the wisdom shared within these pages, let us remember our responsibility to care for the earth and its diverse inhabitants. May this acknowledgement serve as a reminder of the ongoing work needed to ensure respect, recognition, and justice for all Indigenous Peoples.

We express gratitude for the privilege to live and work on these lands, to share this knowledge, and commit to working towards reconciliation, understanding, and building a more inclusive future.

About Author

Tracy, founder of Indigo Journey and an accomplished social worker and coach, is driven by a profound desire to effect positive change in the world. Tracy brings a unique blend of expertise and empathy to her work.

As a proud mother to two incredible adult children and a loving grandparent, Tracy deeply values the significance of family and connection. Her love for nature draws her to both the breathtaking Australian coastline and the serene forests and mountains in Canada, both of which she calls home. She finds solace and inspiration, in and by the water.

She has dedicated her career to creating a safer, more inclusive world for LGBTQ+ individuals. While her holistic approach involves empowering LGBTQ+ individuals to heal and thrive, she also specialises in providing valuable therapeutic counselling and coaching, education, and practical tools for parents and families.

Her unwavering passion lies in creating safe, supportive, and inclusive spaces where individuals can heal, grow, and connect with their authentic selves and each other.

With her compelling writing style, Tracy shares her profound insights, knowledge, and personal experiences to inspire readers on their own transformative journeys. Her words emanate warmth, compassion, and wisdom, encouraging readers to embrace understanding, acceptance, and love.

As a trusted voice in the field of social justice, Tracy's impactful work resonates deeply with readers, touching their hearts and igniting a desire for positive change. Her writing is a testament to her unwavering dedication to building a more inclusive and supportive future for all.

Join Tracy as she invites you to embark on a transformative journey, where her empowering words and heartfelt guidance will empower you to create a more compassionate and inclusive world.